THE

LARRY

WILDE

TREASURY

OF

LAUGHTER

Jester Press
Half Moon Bay
California

Library of Congress Cataloging-in-Publication Data
Wilde, Larry.
The Larry Wilde treasury of laughter.

Includes bibliographical references.
1. American wit and humor. I. Title. II. Title:
Treasury of laughter.
PN6162.W472   1992   818' 5402 -- dc20   91058604

ISBN 0-945040-01-6 (hardcover) $25.00

Jester Press books are available
at special discounts for bulk purchases,
for sales promotions, premiums,
fund raising or educational use.
For details contact:

Jester Press
116 Birkdale Road
Half Moon Bay
California
94019

ii

Dedication

To Mark Padow, bon vivant,
faultless friend, and a fervently funny fella.

With very special thanks to some very special people: Jane
Jordan Browne, Ed Blissick, Nancy E. DeBolt, Dan Poynter
and Mary Poulos Wilde.

BOOKS BY LARRY WILDE

Hardcover

The Larry Wilde Treasury of Laughter
The Larry Wilde Library of Laughter
The Complete Book of Ethnic Humor
How The Great Comedy Writers Create Laughter
The Great Comedians Talk About Comedy

The "Official" Joke Books

Absolutely Last Polish
Absolutely Last Sex Maniacs
All-America Joke Book
Bedroom/Bathroom
Black Folks/White Folks
Cat Lovers/Dog Lovers
Computer Freaks
   (with Steve Wozniak)
Democrat/Republican
Dirty
Doctors
Executives
Golf Lovers
Golfers
Jewish/Irish
John Jokes
Last Irish
Last Italian
Last Jewish
Last Polish

Last Sex Maniacs
Last Smart Kids
Lawyers
Limericks
Locker Room
Merriest Christmas Humor
More Democrat/Republican
More Doctors
More Jewish/Irish
More Polish/Italian
More Sex Maniacs
More Smart Kids/Dumb Parents
Polish/Italian
Politicians
Rednecks
Religious/Not So Religious
Sick Jokes
Smart Kids/Dumb Parents
Sports Maniacs
Virgins/Sex Maniacs

W.A.S.P

The "Ultimate" Joke Books

Ethnic Humor
Jewish

Pet Lovers
Sex Maniacs

Lawyers

CONTENTS

"What makes people laugh?"
"Anything that is funny."
"But what is funny?"
"Anything that makes people laugh."

HOW TO TELL JOKES
FOR FUN AND PROFIT

Being funny for money.

A bunch of cons at San Quentin met in the recreation hall after dinner for their evening's relaxation. Suddenly one prisoner stood up and exclaimed, "72!" Everybody laughed.

Another inmate got to his feet and called out, "53!" All the men guffawed. A third convict brought down the house just by shouting, "86!"

Weasel McCall, who had recently arrived at the Big House, turned to Lefty Lanier, a lifer, and inquired, "What's going on?"

"We're tellin' jokes!" he replied. "But instead of tellin' a yarn that all the boys already know, we just yell out a number from our joke books. Saves a lot of time."

Anxious to get in good with the guys, Weasel stood up and shouted, "22!" Nothing happened. Again he tried, "17!" Silence. Weasel took Lefty aside and asked, "How come they didn't laugh?"

"Well, kid," said the con, "the jokes are all right but you just don't know how to tell them."

1

The ability to tell funny stories has long been regarded as a unique gift possessed by a very special few. Most authorities agree that it's not a talent with which most people are born. As a result, really good storytellers are as scarce as free drinks in a Scottish saloon. In the hands of the unskilled or untrained, the best of jokes are completely spoiled through poor delivery, bad timing, unnecessary words and the lack of preparation.

The art of telling a funny story or an amusing anecdote can be mastered simply by knowing and applying the proper techniques. Practically anyone can learn these fundamentals.

Comedy is a craft. The techniques used to make people laugh, though not generally known, are nonetheless possible to master. Heretofore, the know-how took long painful years to develop. In show business, some of the more basic procedures were passed along by older veteran comedians to younger aspiring comics. But, by and large, to become a successful professional on the stage or a skilled after-dinner speaker in the banquet halls, one had to learn the tricks of the trade the old-fashioned way — through exhaustive, sometimes heartbreaking experience.

Times have changed. Today education and training grounds are more readily available. Schools and comedy clubs abound nationwide. Many comedy beginners write original gags, but for those who cannot create their own material there are humor anthologies which provide jokes, quips and stories on every conceivable subject (see Humor Bibliography).

For the countless humor lovers who wish to learn how to tell jokes for fun or profit some practical tools are hereby presented. The following elementary rules and guidelines are offered to help hone the skills needed to evoke laughter from an audience.

IT'S ALL IN THE TELLING

The old adage "it's not *what* you say but *how* you say it," is the very essence of communicating humor. Tone of voice is all important. People respond more to the tone than to the words. The funniest joke in the world will not receive its just due when obstructed by poor delivery.

How to Tell Jokes for Fun and Profit

Delivery is the articulating of words in a manner or style that is convincing, authoritative, dramatic and entertaining.

In delivering a joke, listeners respond strongly to the tone used by the joke teller. The storyteller must get the essence of the subject matter across in a simple and direct manner. This is particularly important in verbal communication but especially critical when the goal is to evoke laughter.

BENEFITS OF GOOD DELIVERY

There are at least four major benefits when comedy material is well delivered:

The deliverer commands attention.
An audience becomes totally absorbed in the words used and is mesmerized by the tone in which they are expressed. They eagerly await each word and are caught up in the fervor, sincerity and enthusiasm of the performance. A good delivery captures attention and holds it.

Intimacy is established with the audience.
Good delivery conveys authority. If the words are convincing, exciting and entertaining, the audience is won over and they are anxious to hear every detail. A smooth, polished delivery establishes a closer rapport with the audience and makes listening a pleasureful experience.

The audience laughs more easily.
When people are induced to listen closely because of *how* something is said they automatically absorb *what* is said more easily. It is vital that the speaker use every available device to insure that listeners understand each word. When clear comedic thoughts are expertly communicated the audience will respond. Good delivery paves the way to laughter.

3

Competency is conveyed.

The audience senses that the speaker knows what he or she is doing. Self-assurance is perceived and the humorist gains respect. People willingly dismiss whatever reservations or doubts they might have had. They feel safe and comfortable. The performer becomes their leader, their guide, their guru, a person they can admire.

An audience will eagerly and anxiously surrender its emotions to someone they trust. A strong, dynamic style captivates an audience. It conveys confidence and believability. But most of all, good delivery makes a statement: I am competent, skilled and gifted.

Of course, you just don't wake up one morning having automatically acquired a good delivery. It doesn't happen overnight. It takes years of concentrated effort and continuous rehearsal. However, there is a way to speed up the process by learning and practicing four basic techniques essential in achieving a good delivery: gestures, body movement, facial expressions and vocal variety.

ELEMENTS OF GOOD DELIVERY

Gestures.

The calculated use of hands and arms is invaluable. Pointing a finger, making a fist, holding up the hands or waving the arms at an appropriate moment helps to accentuate the meaning of what you're trying to convey. The gesture is the speaker's picture-painting device, and the premier technique for reaching across the distance between you and the audience. Gestures demonstrate. They dramatically illustrate and emphasize what you are saying. Gesticulating at the right time helps generate bigger laughs.

For a real education in the art of gesturing, watch the great pantomimist, Marcel Marceau. After an evening with this French virtuoso, you'll very quickly understand and appreciate the importance of movement. It is the body's silent articulation.

Body movement.
The acts of posturing, posing, strutting, staggering, shrugging, bending, kneeling, leaning or bowing assist in creating the word pictures you are trying to paint. Body language is the message behind the words. It's been said that true communication is :
> 7% words,
> 38% voice quality,
> 55% body language.

Facial expressions.
The simple raising of an eyebrow, squinting, sneering, smiling, grinning, any use of facial muscles provides an additional dynamic dimension to what you are saying. You help the joke with action. An animated, expressive face prompts listeners to laughter.

Vocal variety.
Lowering or raising the pitch of your voice, speaking louder or softer, saying something sweetly, respectfully, angrily, shouting, whispering or pausing for effect are attention getters. Imagine how flat music would sound if it had no dynamics — no exciting crescendos or breathless pianissimos. In the same manner that dynamics add fire to music, vocal variety adds excitement to the spoken word. A well-modulated voice is stimulating and evocative, whereas a dull monotone speaker is a boring communicator with a ho-hum delivery.

Spending a few minutes every day on perfecting each of these techniques will lead to a more polished and professional delivery. However, there's still one other technical skill that is absolutely vital to mastering the art of storytelling, and that is — timing.

Timing is the art of delivering words, phrases and sentences in a rhythmic or varying tempo with calculated emphasis in order to heighten their effectiveness.

Joke telling requires good timing. Without it the laugh could be completely lost. On the other hand, when the audience is laughing, if you start speaking before the laugh begins to diminish, the response will be shortened, cut off. This is known as "stepping on the laugh."

Good timing gets good results. Jack Benny, perhaps more than any other comedian, was the recognized master of this technique. In the interview with Jack for my book, *The Great Comedians Talk About Comedy,* I asked him to offer his thoughts on timing.

"A good joke without timing means nothing," Jack replied. "Very often good timing is not so much knowing when to speak but knowing when to pause."

The same question to Bob Hope produced this reply: "At times I have good material, and at other times I have great material, but I know how to cover up the merely good and make it sound great by timing."

POSITIVE EFFECTS OF GOOD TIMING

Listeners comprehend more easily.

Everyone has a natural speech pattern, cadence, or rhythm, just as music has tempo. Once the audience is in sync with your particular cadence they respond more easily. Changing your rhythm abruptly is jarring. When the delivery is rushed or words are out of sync the audience loses the point. If they don't quite understand, the laugh will be sacrificed. Good timing assures the inside track to the listener's brain.

Interest is aroused.

The way in which something is said directly affects how the listener responds. When speech tempo is varied significant pauses employed at the proper points, words are underscored and the listener sees mental images more clearly. Good timing makes any speaker, even a novice, more colorful, appealing and entertaining.

The illusion of spontaneity is created.
The way in which one delivers words, phrases or whole sentences should give the impression that they are being uttered for the first time. To help the audience believe what is being said, speech must sound fresh and natural — not stale and rehearsed like a classroom recitation. Timing a joke is like dancing a waltz — the performer must be smooth and graceful and have a feel for the tempo.

Professionals make humor look effortless. But they rehearse constantly to insure that their timing is flawless, relaxed and comfortable. The preceding physical and verbal devices, when properly applied, help to cue the laughter response in listeners.

However, making a large group of people laugh is never easy. There are many intangibles that can mitigate against success. Sometimes there is a poor sound system. The room in which the show or the program is being held can be too warm or too cold. The seating might be badly arranged, perhaps the audience has difficulty seeing or hearing. The lighting may be insufficient, or — the performer's worst nightmare — the audience might be tired, indifferent, drunk or rowdy.

Any or all of these distractions, which are often beyond the performer's control, can dramatically stem the flow of laughter and cause disappointing crowd reaction.

But there are other reasons within the performer's control that cause unqualified and untrained joke tellers to get less than the laugh a funny story deserves. They are often unaware of the causes for not getting a favorable reaction. The following are solutions for some common mistakes:

HOW TO GET BIGGER LAUGHS

Don't rush the punchline.
Establish a natural, easy tempo and stick with it. Suddenly rushing the punchline unduly jars the audience. Speaking too quickly loses listeners and they might not catch what is being said. This abbreviates the laugh. The

7

punchline should always be delivered in the same tempo and rhythm as the rest of the joke.

Uses pauses for effect.

Pauses are part of good timing if used judiciously. Stopping in the wrong place will throw off the tempo you've begun, disrupt the flow, make the audience uncomfortable and ultimately lessen the laugh. Always pause at a point that is natural or that enhances the sensible phrasing of the joke. Smart, calculated pauses are absolutely indispensable to getting bigger laughs.

Speak with energy.

Enthusiasm is infectious. A passionate discourse is a foolproof way to enthrall a crowd. Conversely, an audience becomes bored quickly with a flat, dull, colorless speaker. A spirited voice is always more interesting. Speaking with energy insures that the audience will hear every word. If they can't hear what is being said how can they be expected to laugh?

To make sure that I'm clearly heard, I always turn up the sound system to the point just before feedback, then I lay back from the michrophone at least six inches. By doing this I have greater control over the volume, and my delivery.

Articulate clearly.

Enunciate plainly and distinctly so that each member of the audience can grasp every word that is being uttered. Slurred or mumbled words confuse listeners. Good diction boosts the chances of getting big laughs. Speaking so that everyone can follow from point to point insures that nobody will ever be forced to ask, "What did he say? I didn't get it."

Shakespeare offers sound advice: Hamlet instructs a group of traveling actors who arrive at the castle to perform before the king and queen, "Speak the speech, I pray you, trippingly on the tongue ... Nor do not saw the air too much with your hand but use all gently ... you must acquire and beget a temperance that may give it smoothness."

In other words ...

Don't over gesticulate.

The use of gestures is essential to getting the point of the joke across but overdoing it can be distracting. When coordinating movements of the hands to correspond with words it is best to remember that less is more.

Don't laugh at your own jokes.

Chuckling before or after delivering a joke is unnecessary and unwise. Let the listener be the judge if the story is amusing. Laughing at the punchline will not help the audience think it's funny.

Avoid insult, put-down or off-color material.

They never pay. As long as there is a possibility of hurting somebody's feelings the performer loses. A cheap laugh sacrifices good will. No matter how funny the joke is or how much the audience chuckles, if someone has been offended, the effort ultimately fails. Stay away from sensitive subjects such as racial slurs, anti-gay remarks, extreme filth and humor that degrades women. The best axiom is: if in doubt — leave it out. A firm rule should be: keep it clean. Never tell a story that might offend.

Talk less — say more.

Nothing stands in the way of a good laugh more than a joke that is wordier than necessary. The fewer the words the greater the laugh. The size of the laugh you get is inversely proportional to the number of words used to reach the punch line. Once again the adage *less is more* becomes the rule.

Note the number of words used in some of the greatest works ever written:

The Lord's Prayer — 56 words,
23rd Psalm — 118 words,
Ten Commandments — 297 words,
United States Department of Agriculture Regulation Governing the Price of Cabbage — 15,629 words.

This classic story is a good illustration:

Marjorie became attracted to the art of flower arrangement. When she entered competitions she didn't do well and finally asked one of the judges for advice. The kindly old judge gave her three envelopes to be opened one at a time when she next tried her hand.

The message in the first envelope read: Take out half of your flowers and rearrange the rest.

9

*Marjorie did so. The second message was like the first:
Take out half of your flowers and rearrange the rest.
She did as requested. The third message was the same.
Marjorie followed instructions and won the first prize.*

These final words from the Bard of Avon: "Brevity is the
soul of wit."

Rehearse. Rehearse. Rehearse.

Tell your joke in front of a mirror. Practice it out loud.
Repeat it to friends, family or co-workers — anybody who
will listen. Repeat it over and over again until you can tell it
without the slightest hesitation or mistake. Keep doing it
until it becomes as natural as breathing and you feel
comfortable and at ease.

Record it on audio tape exactly the way you would tell it
before an audience. Play it back. Listen to it carefully and
objectively. Be hyper-critical of your work. Make sure
you've followed the rules you've learned. Then, record it
and check it again. Do this a half dozen times for each joke.

Milton Berle says, "Security is knowing your lines."

Practicing the craft of comedy is the ultimate training
ground. Groucho Marx wrote in his autobiography,
Groucho and Me, "All good comedians arrive by trial and
error." Anyone who wants to flourish as a professional
funny person can only accomplish this goal by constant and
disciplined drill.

Stand-up comedians sound spontaneous precisely
because they are not. The material they use is constantly
honed, refined and rehearsed.

Doing your comedy homework will enable you to
approach the audience without fear.

If you'd like to become an accomplished joke teller, there
really are no shortcuts. You must do the required work.
Watching professional athletes before a game is a great
lesson in what is required to become especially proficient at a
particular skill.

Before each game baseball players practice fielding,
throwing and batting. They do loosening up exercises. They
run sprints. And they do this before *every* contest whether
they're regulars or will sit on the bench throughout the entire

game. They do it because they know the importance of practice. They have to be ready, prepared to participate at a moment's notice.

The following dictum is prominently displayed above my desk as a constant reminder:

Failure to prepare is preparation for failure.

TEN TIPS TO INCREASE HUMOR SKILLS

Most joke tellers don't necessarily want to become professional humorists or stand-up comedians, but having a keen insight into the mechanics and techniques used to make people laugh provides a greater appreciation of the craft. Here are some helpful hints that will serve as a guide toward a better understanding of the mysterious and magical world of evoking laughter.

1. Become familiar with humor classics.

The great humor writers are an invaluable source for educating the funny bone. Start with the works of Mark Twain, Robert Benchley, James Thurber, Dorothy Parker and George S. Kaufman, along with playwrights George Bernard Shaw, Henrik Ibsen, Nikolai Gogol and Oscar Wilde.

Studying their writing styles, comic characters and chuckling at the comedic insights of these celebrated writers offers a magnificent foundation, a basis from which to derive a better perception and comprehension of comedy.

Every single funny thought that the mind absorbs is an added stroke to the vast storehouse of one's humor capacity. Furthermore, reading the humor classics enriches and refreshes the soul.

2. Review books on comedy technique.

Until just a few years ago there weren't any books on how to go about becoming a comedy professional. Fortunately, volumes are available now that are filled with information and cover a myriad of details.

Especially informative are Steve Allen's perceptive explorations into comedy and comedians, *The Funny Men, Funny People* and *More Funny People* as well as his *How To Be Funny.* Comedy writer Gene Perret's *How To Hold Your Audience With Humor* is a must. And *Comedy Techniques for Writers and Performers* by former advertising exec Mel Helitzer is very worthwhile.

For a more complete selection of resources see the Humor Bibliography.

3. Watch comedians at work.

Many of the finer points in performing comedy can be learned by observing the pros. Watching them objectively is a golden opportunity to absorb and adapt techniques.

Study their methods. See how they set up the joke. Pay close attention to delivery. Observe their facial expressions, mannerisms and body language. Zeroing in on the harmonious movements of a skilled comedy technician is a sure way to improve your body's vocabulary.

Take in the audience reaction to the material used by the comedian. Measure how funny the material is. How the audience reacts to it. Note the various crowd responses to different kinds of jokes.

Tape the televised appearances of the best comedians and study the tapes. See how they respond to getting small laughs, big laughs or no laughs at all.

Get in the habit of studying the work of each comedian. Learn to analyze and critique the performance. Developing a critical eye and ear will help you become more objective when analyzing your own techniques.

Super star Danny Kaye wasn't just a funny man, he was a great entertainer. The first time I saw him perform on a New York stage it was hard to believe that anyone could be so versatile. He sang, danced, told jokes and even turned the audience into his own personal choral group.

I went back to watch Kaye ten days later and discovered, to my amazement, that he did the exact same act, word for word, line for line, gesture for gesture. Every movement was carefully and artfully choreographed. There was not a single wasted motion or extraneous word. The performance was identical to the first one I saw yet it seemed fresh and spontaneous. Sheer genius.

Over the years, I watched Danny Kaye perform in person 27 times. The words were always the same, the gestures repeated, the movements exact. I marveled at his incredible talent. During each performance I mentally catalogued his comic delivery, the timing, the change of tempos in the songs, the audience rapport, his vocabulary, the gestures, even the clothes he wore. I was studying a master in the hope of acquiring my Ph. D. in comedy. What an education!

4. Listen to comedy tapes.

Pay close attention to the delivery and timing of the performer. Listen carefully to the vocal nuances used in communicating the material to the audience. Play the tape over and over in order to become completely familiar with the comedian's rhythm and his or her style. You'll soon recognize many of the techniques previously discussed.

5. Practice gestures before a mirror.

Tell a joke or story that you plan to use in front of an audience and watch your hand motions. When you've come upon a natural gesture that looks good with a particular phrase or sentence lock it in. Try to do it the same way every time. Make it part of your routine. Gestures are choreography. When they fit what you're saying use them over and over again.

After a speaking engagement recently in Pennsylvania, an elderly couple approached me at the podium. "We really your enjoyed your presentation," said the husband with a broad grin. "My wife wears a hearing aid so she usually doesn't like speakers."

"But I understood every word you said," added the woman. "I especially enjoyed the way you use your hands. They're so expressive."

I couldn't help remembering when I first started to perform. Gestures were a big problem for me. I felt uncomfortable using my hands. They always seemed to get in my way. It was frustrating but I knew that if I was going to stay in show business I'd have to do something about it.

I bought a record album of Strauss waltzes and as the music blared from a little portable phonograph, I stood in front of a mirror and conducted the orchestra. My hands were awkward and clumsy. The arm movements looked lumbering and ungraceful. I practiced hours on end but as the weeks wore on I still felt uncomfortable. It was tiring and boring.

Then one afternoon months later, I began to feel a freedom when I gestured. It was relaxed and effortless. My arms had a mellifluous movement. I realized then I'd finally gained control of my hands. From that day on I was comfortable gesturing.

The couple in Pennsylvania reminded me of my effort in front of the mirror all those years ago and made it seem very worthwhile.

6. Take acting classes.

Reading plays, learning lines and acting out scenes with other actors helps enormously to cultivate communication skills. These exercises demand concentration, they improve memory and require a wide range of vocal expression as well as body language. Learning to relate to other people on stage provides practice in eye contact and encourages a range of emotions to be expressed. Rehearsing and delivering the exact lines of a play as the playwright intended is invaluable discipline.

This priceless experience will nurture your talent, boost your confidence and equip you with know-how that will last a lifetime.

7. Join a dance class.

In order to use the body effectively when expressing ideas or feelings, you must have control of it. Modern dance and ballet teach discipline. There must be no wasted motion. Every professional actor at one time or another takes dance classes. Even athletes are often found along side ballerinas studying the ballet to strengthen their legs, add dexterity and gain ease of movement.

8. Get voice training.

Speaking to audiences frequently requires a strong, healthy voice, one that will stand up with constant use and won't break down when a cold or virus strikes and you must work. Knowing how to use the voice properly is just one more tool to help communicate effectively. These basic techniques are learned from a competent voice coach. Get one.

9. Read a joke book 15 minutes every day.

Prolific humor columnist Art Buchwald told me that each day before he begins work he likes to prime the pump by reading jokes.

The more joke plots you know the more ideas you will get to create your own material. You'll learn construction. You'll discover the many different joke forms (one-liners, quips, puns, limericks, stories, etc.) and where to fit them in your routine.

Then there's the advantage of building up your own joke file. Save all the gags you like and list them under specific headings or subjects.

Get in the habit of telling one new joke every day to anybody who'll listen. Recounting the same joke to twenty people makes you more familiar with it. Delivery is improved with each telling. Timing is perfected. This is a safe opportunity to experiment, to find out if the joke is funny — and if it works for you. Best of all, you are practicing your craft.

10. Seek guidance from a pro.

Especially if you wish to be a paid performer. Athletes are groomed by coaches. Teachers train musicians. Pros seek pointers from other pros. The more proficient you want to become the more you need instruction and direction to enhance and polish your skills.

After switching careers — from stand-up comedian to motivational humorist — I sought guidance in putting together a suitable program for the speaking profession. I worked with veteran comedy writer and producer Milt Josefsberg (*All In The Family, Laverne and Shirley,* Lucille Ball, Jack Benny, Bob Hope, et al) on my keynote speech.

I gave him the script and a tape of a live talk. He made many suggestions for trimming sentences, cutting words and adding amusing lines to stories that would make them funnier.

Long hours were spent perfecting the script, making subtle changes that most people would never even notice. In addition to improving the comedic quality of my presentation, Milt provided me with a better handle on the kind of humor required of me from the platform.

Even more valuable were his enthusiastic comments and encouragement. These kind words, coming from a master of the craft whom I highly respected, boosted my morale and gave me a feeling of accomplishment.

No polished professional ever got that way without the counsel and objectivity of other pros.

These tips and pointers are meant to be time-savers, simple suggestions to help pave the way toward achieving greater success in the art of storytelling. Making people laugh is an honorable and noble undertaking. From the medieval days of the court jester to the contemporary antics of Robin Williams, funny people have nurtured and contributed to one of the world's greatest natural resources — laughter. The work is demanding but the rewards are sublime for those who devote their lives to it.

In his book *All My Best Friends,* George Burns writes, "There is nothing that feels as good as standing on stage and hearing the laughter and applause of an audience."

May that joy be yours in abundance.

LARRY WILDE

PLATFORM PERSIFLAGE

It takes me three weeks to prepare
for an impromptu speech.
— MARK TWAIN

A lecturer was speaking to a Sacramento women's club. His subject: What's Wrong with the Movies Today.

"The one I saw last night," he finally concluded, "is the worst yet. It includes murder, rape, arson, cannibalism and perversion. If anything justifies censorship, this shocking deplorable, immoral picture does. All right now, do you have any questions?"

"Yes," cried out three women simultaneously. "Where is it playing?"

**Always leave your audience
before your audience leaves you.**

A Stuffed Fish Mounted On The Wall With This Sign:

> If I had kept my
> mouth shut
> I wouldn't be here.

SPEAKER:	A horrible thing has happened. I've just lost my wallet with five hundred dollars in it. I'll give fifty dollars to anyone who will return it.
VOICE IN REAR:	I'll give one hundred dollars!

    The program chairperson of most organizations is usually a volunteer with hardly any experience in putting together a successful meeting. A Florida dinner club engaged a good speaker and a large hotel meeting room. When the speaker arrived, he seemed to be in a crabby frame of mind.

    He beckoned the chairman and said, "I would like to have a glass of water on my table, if you please."

    "To drink?" asked the chairman.

    "No," said the speaker sarcastically, "when I've been speaking a half hour, I do a high dive."

    The program chairperson of an Albuquerque women's club walked up to the speaker after the meeting and said, "You were so much better than the speaker we had last week — he spoke for an hour and said nothing. You did it in fifteen minutes."

**Little kids who talk too much
usually grow up to be public speakers.**

Platform Persiflage

Half the world is composed of people who have something to say and can't and the other half who have nothing to say and keep saying it.

— ROBERT FROST

Edgar Whitney was attending his Ohio State class reunion and after dinner, he was called to the lectern. As he walked up the emcee said, "We are all very proud of Ed Whitney. We hear that he has made five million dollars in the lumber business right here in Ohio." The emcee then handed the mike to Edgar and asked him to say a few words.

Whitney took the mike, cleared his throat and said, "I guess somebody must've gotten a few facts screwed up. Most of what you heard is true but there are one or two things that I'd like to correct. Actually it wasn't the lumber business, it was the oil business. It wasn't here in Ohio, it was in Texas. And it wasn't five million dollars, it was only five hundred thousand. And, it wasn't me, it was my brother. And he didn't make it, he lost it."

AFTER-DINNER SPEAKING

The art of saying nothing at length.

Booth Tarkington, the well-known American writer, was once asked to act as master of ceremonies at the burial of a deceased bigwig politician. "Where's he being buried?" inquired Tarkington.

"He's going to be cremated," was the answer.

"You don't want a master of ceremonies," urged the writer. "You want a toastmaster."

A speaker who does not strike oil in ten minutes should stop boring.

In South Carolina a temperance lecturer stood before a jam-packed Sunday-come-to-meeting crowd. He shouted, "Here's an argument drawn from nature. If you was to lead a donkey up to a pail of water and a pail of beer, which would he drink?"

"The water," shouted a Charlestonian.

"Right. Why?"

"Because he's an ass," said the Southerner.

It was a long evening. There had been many speakers and many words. Finally it was George Bernard Shaw's turn as the last speaker. After the applause subsided, he remarked, "Ladies and gentlemen, the subject may not be exhausted. But we are."

And he sat down.

A noted cable television newscaster on a trip to China was invited to speak before a Chinese audience. As he spoke, he noticed a man in a corner writing on a blackboard in Chinese.

The writer wrote fewer and fewer characters and then half way through the speech, he finally stopped completely. When the newscaster had finished speaking, he asked the chairman what the writer had been doing.

"Why," said the chairman, "he was interpreting your speech for the members of the audience who do not understand English."

"But," said the speaker, "for the last 20 minutes, he didn't put anything down."

"Oh," said the chairman, "he was only writing the intelligent ideas on the blackboard."

**Some men can speak for an hour
without a note — and without a point.**

"His after-dinner speech was very well received."
"Really? What did he say?"
"He said, 'Waiter, give me the check.'"

Pintor approached the Rotary program chairman and asked to speak to his club.

"Have you ever addressed the public?"

"Oh, yeah. I've addressed thousands of people in Madison Square Garden."

"What did you say?"

"Peanuts! Popcorn! Pepsi Cola!"

George Jessel was the consummate banquet speaker. President Harry Truman dubbed him "Toastmaster General of the United States." Jessel was often called upon to deliver the eulogy at funerals. In fact, he did so many of these, people used to claim the most-feared question in show business was George asking, with an anxious look in his eye, "So, how are you feeling?"

Jessel loved speaking at funerals. Sometimes he did two in one day, and was superb. Georgie and Sam Bernard, the great actor, had been good friends, and when Bernard died Georgie gave a beautiful, very touching eulogy at the funeral. Everybody was crying. Three days later Georgie walked into the Friars Club wearing his formal striped pants again. Whenever you saw Jessel in those trousers it meant he was appearing at another funeral. "Who died?" asked his old friend, George Burns.

"Louie Mann," said Jessel, referring to the theater chain owner. "I'm on my way over to the funeral."

"I don't get it," said Burns. "A few days ago you told me you didn't like Louie Mann."

"I didn't," explained George, "but I've got some great stuff left over from Sam Bernard."

God gave eloquence to some — brains to others.

Suddenly, it was over. And now that he was finished and the facts were before them, there existed a vast quiet. Not one member of the huge audience stirred. It was a silence pregnant with possibilities; anything might be born of a calm such as that. But strange to say, absolutely nothing happened. They were all asleep.

"I'm going to make this short," said the speaker, "because it's been said that the number one fear of most people is having to make a speech. The number two fear is having to listen to one."

Bob Hope has made some telling points from the stage, making audiences laugh while doing it. He says he used to play towns where the theaters were so small that, in one of them, he took a bow "and some guy in the balcony tried to comb my hair. Fortunately," he added, "the usher made him put the axe back on the wall."

It was in one of these towns that Bob spoke before an audience that just sat there and stared. They seemed interested, but the most he could raise out of them was a grave, sad smile every now and then. He tried every trick in his book, and by the time he got off the stage he was dripping sweat from every pore. And the audience had not laughed a single time.

Backstage, he found a senior citizen waiting for him. "Mr. Hope," the old guy said, "I just wanted to come back and tell you how much we enjoyed your show."

Before Bob could say anything the old man went on: "I tell you, it was all we could do to keep from bustin' out with laughter right there in the meeting."

**Blessed are they who have nothing
to say and cannot be persuaded to say it.**

22

Platform Persiflage

A speaker talking for more than two hours said, "I'm sorry I spoke so long — you see I haven't got a watch."

"Yes," shouted someone from the audience, "but there's a calendar in back of you."

Speechwriters provide a much-needed service but pay a heavy price for their expertise. They must understand the speaker's temperament, take the responsibility for failure but get no credit for the success. A New York writer wrote speeches and articles for a famous millionaire egomaniac, who not only underpaid the writer, but continually subjected him to incessant abuse.

The ghostwriter finally had his revenge. He provided the egomaniac with a long speech to read at a big convention. The millionaire read the first eight pages of the speech, but when he turned to page nine in the middle of a sentence, he found only these words: "OKAY, YOU POMPOUS ASS, NOW YOU'RE ON YOUR OWN."

A city councilman had a habit of rambling on when he spoke. One evening he visited a neighborhood homeowner's association meeting but found only ten people in attendance. Afterward he approached the association president and asked, "Didn't you tell them I was speaking tonight?"

"No, I didn't," said the president, "but word must have leaked out anyway."

An inexperienced speaker arose in confusion after dinner and murmured stumblingly:

"M-m-my f-f-friends, when I came here tonight only G---G-G-God and myself knew what I was about say to you — and now only God knows!"

Speeches are like babies;
easy to conceive but hard to deliver.

**When some speakers end
their talks there is a great awakening.**

"Do you know what it is to go before an audience?"
"No, I spoke before an audience once, but most of it
went before I did."

Pastor Colby visited a Sunday school and was called
upon to address the children. Thinking he might be clever,
he asked this question: "What would you do before so many
bright boys and girls who expect a speech from you, if you
had nothing to say?"
"I'd keep quiet," replied a small boy.

Lord Tewksbury, while in Washington, D.C., attended a
lavish banquet. He heard the master of ceremonies give the
following toast:
"Here's to the happiest moment of my life,
Spent in the arms of another man's wife — my mother."
"By jove," said the Englishman to himself, "I must
remember to use that back home."
Some weeks later in London, he attended a church
luncheon and was asked to give a toast. In thunderous tones
he addressed the crowded room:
"Here's to the happiest moment of my life,
Spent in the arms of another man's wife —"
After a long pause the crowd began to grow restless,
glaring at the speaker. A friend sitting next to Tewksbury
whispered, "You had better explain yourself quickly."
"By jove," blurted the Briton, "you will have to excuse
me. I forgot the name of the bloomin' woman."

**Public speakers should speak up
so they can be heard, stand up so they
can be seen, and shut up so they can be enjoyed!**

Platform Persiflage

**Some speakers would be
enormously improved by laryngitis.**

The speaker was getting tired of being interrupted. "We seem to have a great many fools here tonight," he exclaimed. "Wouldn't it be advisable to hear one at a time?"

"Yes," said a voice. "Get on with your speech."

The foreign history expert was waiting for the lunch to end so that he could be introduced. As the tables were being cleared the program chairman noticed that the room was filled with lively conversation. He turned to the speaker and said, "The crowd sure seems to be having a wonderful time. Should I let them enjoy themselves a little while longer or should I introduce you now?"

After a lecturer had overstayed his allotted time on the podium by a full forty minutes, a sore-bottomed but silver-tongued program chairman consoled other disgruntled patrons with this reminder:

> It's never so bleak
> But it couldn't be bleaker,
> There might have been
> A second speaker!

And then he added these lines by R. Cheney:

> Charm and wit and levity
> May help you at the start;
> But in the end it's brevity
> That wins the public's heart.

**In making a good speech
it is all right to have a train of
thought as long as you also have a terminal.**

Bigelow, a computer software marketing V.P., was sent on ahead to Japan to speak to all the Tokyo company reps. After lunch he stood up and began trying to communicate with his Asian audience. Bigelow was not a terribly good speaker. He tried to brighten up his talk with jokes but they were ponderous and unnecessarily drawn out. Even though the interpreter had to translate his remarks, the Japanese salesmen laughed uproariously at every amusing comment he made. He was elated.

Afterward he said to the interpreter, "Gosh, these guys were a great audience."

"Oh, yes.Your stories were too long to explain. So I say to them, 'Mr. Bigelow told a joke, everyone please laugh!'"

Professor Peabody, a well-known California scientist, was asked to travel throughout the state and speak to various groups in the scientific community about his latest discovery. In a limousine driven by Chatsworth, a chauffeur, he set out on a speaking tour.

Each night Chatsworth stood in the rear of the auditorium, listening carefully to the professor's speech and then to the question and answer period.

After two weeks the chauffeur said, "I can recite your whole lecture by heart."

"Really?" said the professor, excitedly. "Wouldn't it be great fun to change places?"

"What do you mean?"

"Tonight, you wear my suit. I'll wear your uniform and stand in back of the auditorium. You go up on stage and give my speech."

That night the chauffeur gave a brilliant speech. Then came the Q. and A. period. The questions were the same as they had always been and Chatsworth answered them perfectly. Then a woman asked something new.

Chatsworth paused, "That question is so easy I'm going to let my chauffeur in the back answer it."

A good speech has a good beginning and a good ending, both kept close together.

Platform Persiflage

Churchill was always rewriting his speeches until he had to give them. But that's where my similarity to Churchill ends.

— ADLAI STEVENSON

A small gathering sat in a chapel to pay their last respects to a departed friend. Several people got up and extolled the virtues of the deceased. Then the minister delivered a heart-warming eulogy. When he finished he said, "Is there anyone else who would like to say a few words?"

When no one responded a well-dressed man in back of the room stood up and said, "Well, if nobody wants to speak, I'm from Merrill Lynch and I'd like to say a few words about tax free bonds."

When a successful public speaker was asked the secret of his popularity, he said it was really quite simple. "I tell them what I am going to tell them, then I tell them what I told them I was going to tell them, and then I tell them what I have told them."

Returning from the annual Alabama political conference, the small town mayor told a cohort that he had just heard a born orator.

"What do you mean by a born orator?"

"Well," replied the politico, "you and ah would say that two and two make four. But the born orator would say, 'When in the course a human events it becomes necessary and expedient ta coalesce two integers and two other integers, the result — ah declare it boldly and without fear or favor — the result, by a simple, arithmetical calculation termed addition, is four.' That, suh, is a born orator."

Oratory is the power to talk people out of their sober and natural opinions.

27

I believe I shall never be old enough to speak without embarrassment when I have nothing to talk about.
— ABRAHAM LINCOLN

Whittesly returned to the office from the company's annual meeting. "Anything different this year?" asked a colleague.

"Yes," said Whittesly, "we had one of those professional motivational speakers. He was very clever. He didn't have anything to say but he mixed it up with the rest of his speech so you wouldn't notice it."

It was a bitter election campaign, and the Congressman running for reelection was in a mad hurry. He was rushing from his office to address a meeting. On his way down the hall he was stopped by a friend who asked, "Well, what do you think about the political situation now?"

"Don't bother me!" screamed the candidate irritably. "I've got to talk. This is no time to think."

When a woman asked Hubert Humphrey if he would address a large gathering, the famous statesman replied, "Madam, I suffer when I don't."

The master of ceremonies kidded Humphrey at a New York testimonial dinner: "Vice President Humphrey is not an orator, he's a speaker. You say 'Hello' to him, and he says, 'I'm so glad you asked me that!'"

I've never thought my speeches were too long — I've enjoyed all of them.
— HUBERT H. HUMPHREY

Platform Persiflage

Say what you have to say and the first time you come to a sentence with a grammatical ending — sit down.
— WINSTON CHURCHILL

A reporter returned to the office after covering a speech by the paper's favorite candidate. "What did our man have to say?" asked the old editor.

"Nothing," said the reporter.

"Well, keep it to a column," replied the editor.

If all the people who sit
through after-dinner speeches were
lined up three feet apart, they would stretch.

Granger found himself seated at a banquet next to Chen Loo Wing, an important Chinese diplomat. Completely at a loss as to what to say to a Chinese, Granger ventured, "Likee soupee?" Mr. Wing smiled and nodded.

A little later when called upon to say a few words, Chen Loo Wing delivered an eloquent talk in perfect English. He sat down while the applause was still resounding, turned to Granger and said, "Likee speechee?"

A Vermont newspaper reporter paid his respects to a political candidate in this way:

Our newly elected state Congressman spoke at the town hall last night. The best thing that can be said for his address is that it was nothing more than a cowardly attack on the English language.

All work and no plagiarism makes a dull speech.

29

If you don't say anything, you won't be called on to repeat it.

— CALVIN COOLIDGE

The lion sprang upon the bull and devoured him. After he had feasted, he felt so good that he roared and roared. The noise attracted hunters and they killed the lion.

Moral: When you are full of bull, it's better to keep your mouth shut.

SPEAKER: Gentlemen, lend me your ears.
VOICE FROM REAR: You can have mine, and thank heaven I can't hear without 'em.

"Wake that fellow next to you, will you?" snapped the pompous lecturer.

"Better do it yourself, you put him to sleep," barked a man sitting down front.

SECOND WIND

What a speaker gets when he says,
"In conclusion."

Not so long ago the U.S. provided substantial aid to Greece, which was being heavily propagandized by the Communists. The American in charge of our economic mission gave this address: "I am happy to be here tonight with you good citizens of Greece. You Greeks and we Americans have much in common. We like to eat. We like to drink and we like to sit and talk."

The next day the leading Communist paper in Greece announced: "The American Ambassador said that we are just like Americans — gluttons, drunkards and gossips."

Platform Persiflage

Some speakers are born to greatness. Some speakers achieve greatness. Other speakers thrust greatness upon themselves.

— BOB MURPHEY

"I want healthcare reform," roared the politician. "I want tax reform! I want educational reform! I want ..."
"Chloroform," came a voice from the rear.

POLITICIAN: Ladies and gentlemen, please! This is important! But there are so many raucous interruptions I can scarcely hear myself speak.

MAN IN FRONT: Cheer up, Congressman, you ain't missin' much.

A nationally known political analyst agreed, somewhat reluctantly, to address a banquet at an upstate New York nudist colony. When he arrived at the isolated wooded retreat, he was gleefully greeted by dozens of men and women who were completely naked. The program chairman took him to the main building and suggested that he might like to prepare for dinner.

Upstairs in his room the speaker realized that he was trapped and obviously was expected to dress like everyone else. In extreme mental anguish he removed all his clothes. Then hearing the bell for dinner, he marched downstairs as bare as a newborn babe. He discovered that the nudists, in deference to the speaker, were all in black ties and formals.

Some speakers know very little, but they know it fluently.

SPEAKER INTRODUCTIONS

Our speaker tonight is a humble and modest man — and with good reason.

He reminds you of a bee — a humbug.

He talks in stereo — out of both sides of his mouth.

He's a real drip — you can always hear him but can rarely turn him off.

He reminds you of a clarinet — a wind instrument.

Our speaker has not only all of the five senses but he has two more, horse and common.

He could talk his head off and never miss it.

His mouth is so big, he can whisper in his own ear.

He needs no introduction — what he needs is a conclusion.

Meet the sales manager of the Philadelphia Fertilizer Co. He should give a good speech. He's full of his subject.

Every time he opens his mouth, he puts his feats in.

Years ago he was an unknown failure — now he's a known failure.

AFTER BEING INTRODUCED

I notice that one of you is wearing a hearing aid. I'll keep an eye on you, and if I see you turn the volume down, I'll conclude.

Standing here I feel a little like a mosquito who has just landed in a nudist colony. I hardly know where to begin.

Well, your horoscope said something horrible would happen to you today and here I am.

When I sat down after my last speech, the chairperson said it was the best thing I ever did. I'm still trying to figure out exactly what she meant!

I want to thank you for being an attentive audience. I appreciated your applause and laughter — you showed very good judgment.

I can tell already this is going to work out better than the last time I spoke. The sound system buzzed and hummed so badly I had to stop while the electrician checked it out. That wasn't so bad, except that after he fiddled with it for a while, he started telling everybody there was a screw loose in the speaker.

First of all, I want to thank you for the nice greeting you gave me at the airport. It was certainly better than the experience I had recently in another city. The organization I was scheduled to speak for planned to have a motorcade ready to meet me at the airport and escort me to the hotel with great fanfare.

But there was a mix-up. I arrived by an earlier plane and the motorcade wasn't there. After my speech that evening I was approached by the program chairman.

"Sir," said the chairman, "we're powerful sorry that we didn't have the opportunity to escort you into our fair city, but we'll take great pleasure in escorting you out of it."

"Did you ever speak before a big audience?
"Yes."
"What did you say?"
"Not guilty."

The Bozells were poor Mississippi dirt farmers. When their uncle died they approached Reverend Gailard to conduct the funeral service. "We're poor folks," said Bozell. "How much will a funeral cost?"

The preacher said, "I can give you the ten dollar service, the six dollar service, a four dollar service or a fifty cent service or I could do it for free."

"We can't afford $10," said the farmer, "but what's the service like?"

"It's a great service," said the minister. "Everybody in the room will cry. And I will cry too."

"What about the six dollar service?"

"That's good too," said the preacher. "Half the people in the room will cry, and the other half won't."

"What about the fifty cent service?"

"It's a wonderful service. Half the people will cry and the other half laugh."

"And if you do it for free?"

"Then everybody laughs," pledged the preacher.

**The nice thing about
being a really poor speaker is that you
never have to worry about having an off night.**

CORPORATE CACKLES

A successful executive is one who delegates all responsibility, shifts all the blame, and appropriates all the credit.

"My boy," said the president of a large California recording company, "there are two things that are vitally necessary if you are to succeed in business."

"What are they, Dad?"

"Honesty and sagacity," said the exec.

"What is honesty?"

"Always — no matter what happens or how adversely it may effect you — always keep your word once you have given it."

"And sagacity?"

"Never give your word."

Happiness is a corporate executive who has a wife to tell him what to do — and a secretary to do it.

The president of one of the big computer companies opened his directors meeting by announcing: "All those who are opposed to the plan I am about to propose will reply by saying, 'I resign.'"

EXECUTIVE

A big gun that hasn't yet been fired.

A group of business executives, after deploring the youth of today, turned to sharing stories of their own struggles. After several of the men had given harrowing accounts of their early days in business, Marlowe, who was younger than the others, said: "I had a pretty rough time of it for a while. But when I saw what the score was going to be, I simply worked harder and longer — and got another hundred thousand bucks from my old man."

"What kind of a company do you work for?"
"We're a non-profit organization. We didn't mean to be, but we are."

Howlett was telling Bauer, his jogging buddy, that he was starting a business in partnership with another fellow.
"How much capital are you putting in it?"
"None. The other guy is putting up the capital, and I'm putting in the experience."
"So, it's a fifty-fifty agreement," said the friend.
"Yes, that's the way we're starting out," replied Howlett. "But, you see, I figure in about five years I'll have the capital and he'll have the experience."

Success is relative. The more success the more relatives.

Corporate Cackles

The department head was retiring. Atkins was taking up a collection for a dinner and gift for the old guy. Cole refused to chip in. Atkins argued, pleaded, "There'll be dinner and a prize."

"A prize?" howled Cole. "Why, all I'd like to do is give that air head a good boot in the backside."

"Wow!" exclaimed Atkins, "are you psychic or what? That's the first prize."

MANAGER: Can't understand why the employees don't like me. When I left my last job they gave me a silver tray.

FOREMAN: Don't worry, if you'd only leave here I can guarantee you a gold one.

A labor leader was telling one of his associates about the troubles he was having with his wife. When he finally finished, the associate said, "It may surprise you, but I'd have to agree with your wife."

"What?" exclaimed the labor boss. "I never thought you'd go over to management."

"Do you believe in luck in business?"

"Why, of course. How else do you explain the success of those you don't like."

Vetter and Sertin met in the company cafeteria. "Hey, just read in the business section of the *Chronicle* that a certain V.P. left the firm due to 'philosophical differences' with the CEO," said Vetter. "Mind telling me what those 'philosophical differences' were?"

"Yeah," said Sertin. "That dork wanted to work here and the CEO told him to get out."

Proctor, the chief executive of a large corporation, was a stickler for efficiency. On the spur of the moment he decided to make an inspection tour of one of the company's manufacturing units. As his aides followed him through each department, Proctor glowed with satisfaction. The machines hummed and the men were working in swift cohesiveness.

Suddenly the ears of the CEO were tormented by the sound of whistling from behind a partition. He quickly confronted the whistler, Pete, a young man sprawled lazily in a chair.

"What's your salary?" demanded Proctor.

"Ninety bucks a week," Pete said, as he resumed whistling.

The executive snapped, "Give this boy $180 and get him out of here at once."

"But, Mr. Proctor —" began an assistant.

"You heard me! $180 and out," interrupted the CEO.

Later in the day an accounting department official brought up the subject of the whistler.

"What account shall we charge that $180 to, Mr. Proctor?"

"Payroll, naturally," was the official answer.

"But sir, that boy didn't work for us. He was a messenger waiting for a delivery receipt."

"Dad, what is ethics?" asked the youngster.

The father, a prosperous merchant, pondered for a few moments and said, "Well, son, ethics in business is very important. You know that your uncle and I are in business together. Take today, for instance, a customer came in and bought something worth $10 but by mistake he gave me a $100 bill and then left without waiting for his change. Here son, comes the question of ethics. Should I tell your uncle or shouldn't I?"

Economists now say we move
in cycles instead of running in circles.
It sounds better, but it means the same.

Corporate Cackles

Some companies encourage their employees to use a positive attitude to get what they want — other companies simply assign parking spaces.

"Why do you call that old mule 'Corporation?'" an inquisitive neighbor asked the farmer.

"Because," said the farmer, "this mule gets more blame and abuse than anything else around here, but he still goes ahead and does just what he damn pleases."

Lisbeth made an appointment for an interview with a prestigious Colorado corporation. Sitting before the personnel manager she asked if she could get into the company's well-respected training program.

The pressured exec had been beseiged by applications. "Impossible now!" he said. "Come back in about ten years."

"Would morning or afternoon be better?" quipped the ambitious young woman.

CONSULTANT

A person who knows 182 different
ways of making love, but can't get a date.

Woodbridge and Portman were having a cocktail at the club. "Were you ever fired from a job?" asked Woodbridge.

"Yes," replied Portman. "Matter of fact, one of the most tactful bosses I ever knew fired me from my very first job. He called me in and said, 'I don't know how we're going to get along without you, but starting Monday, we're certainly going to try.'"

If you want a job done, give it to a busy executive. He'll have his secretary do it.

Jeakins started at the firm and became friendly with Burrell, a long-time employee. He asked him, "How do you like it here?"

"There's one advantage our company has," answered Burrell. "Not only do we have a good pension plan, but working here ages you quicker."

BOSS: Your salary is a personal matter
        not to be divulged to anyone.
NEW EXEC: I won't say a word; I'm just
        as ashamed of it as you are.

"Mr. Butterworth cannot see you," said the secretary. "He has strained his back."

"Look," said the caller, "I didn't come here to wrestle with him. I just want to talk to him."

The salesman asked where the manager's office was located. Bettie at the information desk directed him. "Follow the passage until you come to a little sign that says, 'No Admittance'. Then go upstairs until you see the sign 'Keep Out,' follow the corridor until you see the sign 'Silence,' then just yell."

Walburton sat before the personnel director. "If I take this job, will I get a raise every year?"
"Yes, if you do a good job."
"I knew there was a snag somewhere."

**An executive is one who goes around
with a worried look — on his assistant's face.**

Microchip executives Tobias and Weller were discussing the recession and their sluggish business.

"You know the difference between computers and the *Titanic*?" said Tobias.

"No," said Weller.

"The *Titanic* had entertainment."

CHIEF EXECUTIVE OFFICER

When you are important enough to take
two hours off for lunch and the doctor
limits you to a glass of milk and a cracker.

Scoey Leach developed a reputation for being the best handyman around town. And he made a good living at it. One day he was hired by a corporate exec to paint his house. After some dickering they agreed to a wage of $10 per hour.

The exec returned home late in the afternoon and found Scoey sprawled out under a tree watching another man doing the painting.

"What's the idea, Scoey?"

"Oh, I sublet the job to that fella up on the ladder for $12 an hour."

"But how can you do that? I'm paying you only $10. You're losing two dollars an hour."

"Yeah, I know that," said the handyman. "But it's worth it to be the boss just once in my life."

"How's your new secretary working out?"

"Well, she's okay, but she gets awfully annoyed when she's late to work. It's not that she's conscientious — she's just mad because she missed a coffee break."

**A business is too big
when it takes a week for gossip
to go from one end of the office to the other.**

41

The company president called in his office manager and held out a letter. "Look at that! I thought I told you to hire a new stenographer on the basis of grammar."

"Grammar!" said the startled manager. "I thought you said glamour."

Looking at her own scribbled stenography, Eileen leaned over to another secretary who attended the directors meeting.

"I can't quite remember," she said, "did Mr. Spengler say that we should retire a loan?"

"Not if I can help it," replied the other girl.

Falkner was filling out an application for union membership. "Does this union have any death benefits?"

"Sure does," replied the representative. "When you die you don't have to pay any more dues."

The irate boss called Carlisle, the young office boy, into his office and demanded to know why certain papers had not been delivered to a customer.

"I did the best I could," replied Carlisle.

"The best you could?" said the boss. "Listen, if I had known I was sending a jackass to do this job, I would have gone myself."

A wealthy corporate president, when asked the reason for his success, said, "I never hesitate to give full credit to my wife."

"And how did she help?"

"Frankly," said the millionaire, "I was curious to see if there was any income she couldn't live beyond."

**An economist is a man who knows
more about money than the people who have it.**

42

Malet and Tuttle, two broken-down elderly men, sat on a park bench near Daytona Beach.

"I'm here, I want you to know," said Malet, "because I never took advice from anybody."

"Let's shake hands," said Tuttle, "I'm here because I took advice from everybody."

BIG BUSINESS

A polite form of larceny, founded on the faith
of the stockholders that they, too, will get theirs.

A computer software office manager posted the following notice on the company bulletin board:

To All Employees

Because of increased competition and a keen desire to remain in business, we find it necessary to institute a new policy. Effective immediately, we are asking that somewhere between starting and quitting time, without infringing too much on the lunch period, coffee breaks, rest periods, story telling, ticket selling, golfing, auto racing, vacation planning, and rehashing yesterday's TV programs, that each employee try to find some time to set aside to be known as *THE WORK BREAK.*

**The reason why people who
mind their own business succeed
is because they have so little competition.**

The owner of a large chain of gift shops was going over his books and discovered that Birnbaum, his most trusted employee, had stolen over a million dollars from the firm.

"I don't want a big scandal," said the owner to the crook. "I'll just fire you and forget about the entire matter."

"Why fire me?" asked Birnbaum. "I now have a sixty-foot yacht, a twenty-room vacation mansion in the Berkshires, a Park Avenue townhouse, a brand new 500 SEL Mercedes-Benz, a $30,000 Rolex watch and every other luxury you can think of. I don't need a thing, so you can trust me. Why hire somebody else and have to start all over with him from scratch?"

Hankin had been a company clerk for over twenty-five years. One day he approached the personnel manager with some reluctance.

"I suppose I'd better retire soon," said Hankin. "My doctor tells me that my hearing is going fast. And frankly, I'm beginning to notice that I don't hear what some of the customers say to me."

"Retire?" exclaimed the manager. "Nonsense! I'll just put you in the complaint department."

"Are you looking for work, young man?"
"Not necessarily, but I would like a steady paycheck."

"My husband is employed by a large corporation as an efficiency expert," said Darlene.

"Just what does an efficiency expert do?" asked her new next-door neighbor.

"Well," explained the woman, "when we wives do it they call it nagging."

He is such a steady worker that he is really motionless.

44

Corporate Cackles

**The best time to start planning
your retirement is before the boss does.**

Allenby was visiting an electronics assembly plant and stayed to have lunch with the owner.

"How long has that office boy been working for you?" asked Allenby.

"About four hours," said the boss.

"Four hours!" exclaimed the visitor. "Why I thought he had been here quite a long while."

"Oh, yes," said the boss, "he's been here all right but you asked how long he's been working for me!"

FROM A CHICAGO HELP WANTED AD

A big executive, from 22 to 80. To sit with feet on his desk from ten to four-thirty and watch other people work. Must be willing to play golf every other afternoon. Salary to start: $3,000 a week.
This job isn't really open. It's just that we thought it would be nice to see in print what everybody is applying for.

Elam applied for a job and was told by the manager that the firm was over-staffed. "You could just start me," suggested the applicant. "The little bit of work I'd do wouldn't be noticed."

**A statistician is a nerd who draws a
mathematically precise line from an unwarranted
assumption to a foregone conclusion.**

Morty and Al, two goldbricking office goof balls, were grabbing a smoke in the basement store room. As usual they were trying to avoid the ever-watchful eye of the company personnel director.

"You look exhausted," said Morty, sprawled lazily on some packing cases. "What happened?"

"Well," said Al, "I — no you wouldn't believe it."

"Of course I would."

"No, you wouldn't believe it. You simply couldn't."

"I'd believe it. Tell me."

"Well, I worked very hard today."

"I don't believe it."

Tunick applied for a job in answer to an ad but was told by the manager, "You're much too late. I already have more than a thousand applications here on my desk."

"Well, then," said the young man, "why not employ me to go through them and classify them for you?"

Millar finished filling out a job application and handed it to the personnel director. "We want a responsible person for this job," said the director.

"Well, I guess I'm just the one," said the young fellow. "No matter where I worked, whenever anything went wrong, they told me I was responsible."

"You're fired," said the office manager.

"Who are you going to get to fill my vacancy?" asked the mail room clerk.

"Vacancy?" said the manager. "Believe me, you're not leaving any vacancy."

**An executive is a person who talks
to the visitors while others are doing the work.**

Corporate Cackles

**The big shots are only little
shots who have made the most noise.**

CLOCK

Something they have in an office so you can
tell how late you wish you weren't in the
morning, how early you go to lunch before and
how late you come back after, and how long
before you start stopping work by
stalling along until.

"What's your definition of being successful?"
"Anybody who makes more money than their child at
college can possibly spend."

Klinger and Russe, two upper management wimps, were
chatting over lunch.
"What did the boss say when you told him you were
worried about meeting the quota?"
"Well," replied Russe, "the boss said he had so many
worries that if a new one came up, he wouldn't have time to
worry about it for at least three weeks."

"Why did the foreman fire you, young man?" asked the
prospective employer.
"You know what a foreman does — stands around all
day and watches others work. Well, my foreman got jealous
of me. Seems that some of the workers thought that I was
the foreman."

**An economist is a man who wears
a watch chain with a Phi Beta Kappa
key at one end and no watch at the other.**

The CEO of a machine tooling company called all his employees together on Monday morning for his weekly pep talk. "Gang, I want you to know I'm exactly like you," he began. "I am not always right — but I'm never wrong."

Then he added, "If you have something to complain about, I want you to speak right out — even if it costs you your job."

SUCCESS

Making money so you can pay
off the taxes you wouldn't have to pay
if you didn't have so much money already.

Mrs. Searle, in charge of the annual charity bazaar, stood up before the board of directors and intoned, "I'm happy to announce that this year's ladies' auxiliary bake sale netted a profit exceeding that of IBM, Chrysler, Chevron and American Airlines combined."

EXEC: I really need a raise. Prices keep going up ... food ... clothing ... everything's going up.
CEO: Not everything.
EXEC: Oh, yeah? Name one thing that's not going up.
CEO: Your salary.

"You just can't come in here like this and ask for a raise," said the boss to the new employee. "You've got to work yourself up."

"Oh, I have," he replied. "Look, I'm shaking all over."

The world is full of willing people: those willing to work and those willing to let them.

Corporate Cackles

They were all gathered together in the conference room. Suddenly a hush fell over the group.

"Team, all that time and effort and money has finally paid off!" said the chief engineer. "Now, I wonder if there's an actual market for this?"

Did you hear about the corporate exec who was on the verge of committing suicide until he discovered the cleaning crew had hung the graph behind his desk upside down?

SIGN IN OFFICE

The easiest way to make ends
meet is to get off your own.

Edith and husband Norbert had a knock-down drag-out battle over his inability to earn a better living. She told him that he hadn't been sufficiently explicit with the boss when he had asked for a raise.

"Tell him," she screamed, "that you have seven children, that you have a sick mother you have to sit up with many nights, and that you have to wash the dishes and clean the house because you can't afford a maid."

Several days later Norbert came home from work, stood before his wife and calmly announced that the boss had just fired him.

"Why?" asked Edith.

"He said he thinks I have too many outside activities," explained Norbert.

The fortunate businessman is one
with a business so small he does not have
to bribe government officials to let him alone.

49

PERSONNEL MANAGER:	Do you have any experience?
APPLICANT:	No, I've just finished school.
PERSONNEL MANAGER:	What kind of job are you looking for?
APPLICANT:	I'd like to be some sort of executive. Maybe a vice president.
PERSONNEL MANAGER:	But we already have twelve vice presidents.
APPLICANT:	That's OK. I'm not superstitious.

SUPERVISOR

A person who can bring gaiety, laughter
and joy to the office — just by being absent.

A San Francisco businessman dining at the chic Campton Place met Lee Iacocca in the restroom. "Mr. Iacocca," he gushed, "I'm your greatest admirer. I respect what you've accomplished. I've read your books, I've studied your career, and what success I've had in business comes from emulating you."

"Thank you," said Iacocca.

"Could I ask a favor, please?" said the fan. "I'm sitting with some colleagues. Would you walk by my table, say 'Hello, Randy!' and let me introduce you. It would mean so much to me."

Iacocca reluctantly agreed. He waited for the man to sit down then walked toward his table with a smile on his face.

"Good heavens," said one of Randy's friends, "it's Lee Iococca, and he's heading this way!"

Just then Iacocca arrived at their table and said, "Hello Randy. Introduce me to your friends."

"Could you come back later, Lee!" he snapped. "We're trying to have lunch!"

Dobbs, an efficiency expert, was making the rounds in an office. He asked a clerk, "What're you working on?"

"Nothing at the moment," said the clerk.

Dobbs made note of it and walked to the desk of the next clerk. "What are you working on?"

"Nothing," replied the clerk.

"Aha!" exclaimed the expert, "Duplication!"

OVERHEARD IN EXEC RESTROOM

"I don't think I look 45, do you?"

"No, but you used to!"

Brimfield, a longtime and faithful employee, was complaining to his friend Gerrity that he had been passed up by his boss for an important promotion.

Brimfield boasted, "I know the business, I can handle the job I didn't get, I had a fine attendance record, and there were no blemishes on my conduct or performance."

"What do you think is the reason?" asked his friend.

"I'm just too slow," said Brimfield.

"Too slow? That doesn't seem to me very important for that job. Besides lots of good employees are a little slow."

"Oh, I'm not a slow worker — just too slow to laugh at the boss's jokes."

Clifton and Neff had been partners for years and now Clifton lay dying. Neff stood at his hospital bedside.

"I have a confession to make," said Clifton. "I robbed our firm of $200,000. I sold the secret formula to our competitors. I took the letter from your desk that your wife needed to get her divorce. And I ..."

"It's all right," said his partner. "It was me who poisoned you!"

**A big gun is often a man
of small caliber and an immense bore.**

51

The paycheck is the company's way of saying "Thank you." Most employees, of course, wish they would say it a little louder.

While visiting New York, Lord Buntington met Frimkin, a very successful dress manufacturer.

"How is it," asked the Englishman, "that you New Yorkers get on so well in business? What's the secret of your success?"

"Brains, my dear man, brains!" boasted Frimkin. "The secret is eating herring. It's brainfood. Give me fifty bucks and I'll send you the same gorgeous fish that my wife buys for me. Eat it and I guarantee you'll get smarter."

The English Lord handed over the fifty dollars, and as promised, a herring was sent to his hotel. Next day he met the dress manufacturer again.

"How did you like the fish?" asked Frimkin.

"It was splendid!" replied Lord Buntington.

"Do you feel different in any way?"

"No, I can't really say that I do. But I've been thinking, old chap, wasn't fifty dollars a jolly stiff price for only one little herring?"

"There you are!" replied the New Yorker. "You're getting smarter already."

You can tell some folks aren't afraid of work by the way they fight it.

JUDICIAL JESTS

**The lawyer agrees with the doctor
that the best things in life are fees.**

Counselor Sharpe and Doctor Wentzell met for a business lunch. "Are you sure," said the lawyer, "that you can prove to the satisfaction of the court that my client is absolutely insane?"

"Why certainly," said the M.D. "And what's more, if you are ever in trouble and need my services, I'll do the same for you, too."

Dr. Garr, the town physician, was buying some bread at Baldwin's Bakery. "I hear that Mantel, the lawyer, is sick," said the baker. "How's he doing now?"

"Ah, the poor fellow," said the doctor, "he's lying at death's door."

"That's nerve for you," said the baker. "At death's door and still lying."

"What was the most confusing case you ever had?" the physician asked the barrister.

"Case of champagne," replied the lawyer. "I hadn't got half through it before I was all muddled up."

A young ambitious corporate attorney was explaining to a friend the five secrets of happiness: Money, Money, Money, Money and More Money.

An Arab prince came to Los Angeles for an eye operation and Doctor Ruthaven didn't know what to charge a royal patient. If he overcharged, it would reflect unfavorably on international relationships and good will. On the other hand, if he undercharged, the Prince would feel the operation was not serious enough to have made a trip to the United States.

The specialist checked with members of his staff and was almost ready to settle for $25,000 until one member suggested he consult Brockton, the prince's lawyer, who was handling his royal highness's financial affairs.

"I suggest," said the attorney, "that you specify no particular amount, but that you submit a blank statement with the note: 'A member of the royal family can do no wrong.' Let the prince decide what it is worth."

Ruthaven did as he was advised. He soon received a check for $75,000. Ten days later the doctor received a blank invoice from the prince's lawyer with the note: "The surgeon can do no wrong."

A lawyer was endeavoring to pump some free medical advice out of his doctor.

"Which side is it best to lie on, Doc?"

"The side that pays you the retainer."

Some lawyers are just
like laundries; they lose your
suit but still take you to the cleaners.

Judicial Jests

"My wife should have been a lawyer."
"Why's that?"
"Every time we have an argument and she feels like she's losing, she takes it to a higher court — her mother."

The lawyer fell on a banana skin
His torn clothes made him feel
That, as the legal words explain —
His suit was lost on a peel.

Did you hear about the Kansas City lawyer who believed in reincarnation?
In his will he left everything to himself.

NEWSPAPER AD

Help Wanted: Busy lawyer
seeks alert young woman to
serve as deceptionist.

"I can win this case," Farrell told his client.
"What can I do to help?" asked the client.
"All right, do exactly what I tell you," said the lawyer, "plead insanity."
"Insanity?"
"Yeah — you've got a much better chance of busting out of the nut house than the can."

A good lawyer knows the law;
a clever one takes the judge to lunch.

Salisbury was going over a bill with his lawyer: "I remember having lunch with you but what's this charge here, 'Luncheon advice, $215'?"

"Don't you remember," said the lawyer, "I recommended the roast pork loin with potato puree?"

Minden, a Baltimore lawyer, double-parked his new BMW on the street and left this note under the windshield wiper: "Attorney — inside attending to business."

An hour later when he returned he found this written below: "Policeman — I attended to mine outside."

And on the windshield was a parking ticket.

Newsome was cross-examining a witness about a large rock that came crashing through a plate glass window.

NEWSOME:	How large was the rock that came through the window. Was it as large as your fist?
WITNESS:	Oh, yes, and much bigger.
JUDGE:	Was it as large as my head?
WITNESS:	Yes sir, your Honor. It was as big, but not as thick.

In Japan there is one lawyer for every 15,000 people — as compared to the United States where there is one lawyer to every 1,500. Here's a way to solve the balance of payments problem — they ship us a Toyota, and we ship them a lawyer.

Pratt walked into his partner's office and proudly announced, "I've just landed that big class action law suit for my son."

"But the boy is only three years old."

"I know, but he'll be ready for it by the time I've finished the preliminary work."

Dobson, a recent law school graduate, was trying desperately to make it in private practice, but with little success. One day while sitting in his office contemplating a stack of unpaid bills, he noticed someone grinning at him from a corner chair. "Who are you?" demanded Dobson.

"I am the Devil," said the visitor, "I'm prepared to offer you a deal. I can guarantee that for 50 years you will win all the cases you undertake. You will become internationally famous, the idol of the legal profession, the greatest name in law since Clarence Darrow and Louis Nizer. You will enjoy these benefits for exactly 50 years. Then you will die quietly in your sleep and your soul becomes mine for all eternity."

The lawyer thought for a moment, then demanded, "Okay, what's the catch?"

LAWSUIT

A matter of expense and suspense.

An attorney named Strange was asked what he would like to have inscribed on his tombstone.

"Just put 'Here lies an honest lawyer,'" he said.

"But," said the friend, "that really doesn't tell who it is."

"Sure it does," said the attorney. "Passersby will read it and say, 'that's Strange.'"

The church was jammed as usual for the 11 a.m. service. Preacher Pratley gave his sermon with great conviction and finally concluded, "In time of trial, what brings us the greatest comfort?"

A young attorney rose and shouted, "An acquittal!"

"You seem to have more than the average share of intelligence for a man of your background," sneered the lawyer at a witness.

"If I wasn't under oath, I'd return the compliment," said the witness.

When there are 10 lawyers buried up to their necks in cement what's wrong?

Not enough cement.

Returning to his seat at the L. A. Forum, popcorn in hand, an obese Brentwood divorce attorney leaned over and asked a woman, "Did I step on your feet when I came out?"

"Well," said the woman, prepared for an apology, "as a matter of fact you did."

"Good," he said, "then this is my row."

"How are you getting along in the law business?"

"I have one client."

"Is he rich?"

"He was."

Clarke was questioning his client:

"Did you present a bill to the defendant, Mr. Herbert?"

"Yes I did."

"And when you did this, what did he say?"

"He told me to go to the devil."

"And what did you do then?"

"Why, I came straight to you."

Sal was brought to court and charged with burglary. His wife Teresa was being cross-examined by Nichols.

"Did you know that this man was a burglar when you married him?" asked the lawyer.

"I did," replied Teresa.

"Then why in heaven's name did you marry him?" persisted Nichols.

"Well," said Teresa, "I was gettin' older and didn't want to be left on the shelf. I had the choice between a burglar and a lawyer, so I married the burglar."

"No further questions," said the attorney.

Judicial Jests

He was one of the best lawyers money could buy.
He not only knew the law — he knew the judge, too.

LAW FIRM

Dewey, Cheatham, and Howe

Did you hear about the small town lawyer in the South who was starving?

Then another lawyer moved to town. Three months later they were both rich!

FIRST LAWYER: Possession is nine-tenths
of the law.
SECOND LAWYER: Tried any drug cases lately?

Contreras was in jail for murder, rape, blackmail, and kidnapping. When the court-appointed lawyer went to see him, he had a gleam in his eye.

"I think I found a loophole." said the attorney. "In the case of McDaniel versus Hopkins, March 4, 1897, California Statutes, volume IV, page 346, paragraph 7, I got the answer. Don't worry about a thing, I'll get you out of this murder-rape-blackmail-kidnapping mess. Just do exactly what I say."

"You got it," said the accused.

"I'm leaving for Palm Springs on Sunday," said the lawyer, "and I'll be back Friday. Meanwhile, try to escape."

Broderick, pleading the cause of a young boy, took the child in his arms and presented the child to the jury as a torrent of tears flowed from the boy's eyes. This had a great effect. But the opposing counsel asked the child what made him cry.

"He pinched me," said the youngster.

"Your office is as hot as an oven," said the new client to a young lawyer.

"And that's the way it should be. After all, this is where I make my bread."

RETAINER

The first holdup.

Caulkin and his associate, Blydon, were walking out of a Minneapolis courtroom. "I feel like telling that judge where to get off again," said Caulkin.

"What do you mean, again?"

"I felt like it last week, too."

JUDGE:	You are charged with throwing your mother-in-law out of your fourth-story window.
DEFENDANT:	I did it without thinking, your Honor.
JUDGE:	Yes, but don't you see how dangerous it might have been for anyone passing at the time?

Young Skip was in court on his first offense. The complaint charged that he had stolen ten bicycles. Rosenbloom, his lawyer, made this suggestion to the court. "Your Honor, this is the boy's first offense. If he paid for the stolen articles, would that be acceptable to the court?"

After considerable discussion by the plaintiff and the judge, it was agreed that the case would be dropped.

Then Rosenbloom jumped up and asked, "Should the boy pay for ten bicycles at wholesale or retail prices?"

O'Conner was defending his first client in a murder trial. As he was making his final speech for the defense, he sent a note to a friend, an eminent lawyer present in the court. "What are the chances of my client being acquitted?"

"Keep talking," answered the friend. "The longer you talk, the longer your client has to live."

Judge Tokushima called for a short recess. His Honor then advised the attorney, "Why not recess with your client to give him the benefit of your best advice."

When the trial resumed, the attorney returned to the courtroom without his client.

"Where's the prisoner?" demanded the judge.

"He's gone," answered the lawyer. "That was the best advice I could give him."

The Alabama judge looked at Macon when he took the witness stand and said, "Do you understand what you are to swear to?"

"Yes, sir, I understand. I am to swear and tell the truth, the whole truth and nothing but the truth."

"That's right," continued the magistrate, "and what will happen if you do not tell the truth? Do you know?"

"Well, your Honor," said Macon slowly, "I suspect our side'll win the case."

Two Washington attorneys were busily discussing a prospective client. They were undecided as to whether to accept the case.

"Before we do anything, tell me, has he any money?"

"He's worth in the neighborhood of a million dollars."

"Good. We take the case."

"Really?"

"Why of course! That's my favorite neighborhood," said the attorney.

A debtor on the witness stand cried, "As God is my judge, I do not owe the money."

The judge replied: "He's not. I am. You do."

Whitmore went duck hunting in New Hampshire in the farm country. After some time he shot a duck and was accosted by Farmer Grisby. "You're on private property," shouted Grisby, "and that duck is mine!"

"Nonsense!" said the lawyer. "I shot it while it was flying. Individuals don't own air rights over property. I shot it, I picked it up, I own it."

"That so?" says the farmer. "Out here we solve property issues the old-fashioned way."

"And what is that?"

"First, I kick you in the groin," said Grisby, "then you kick me. We do that until one of us gives up."

Whitmore eyed his hunting boots versus the farmer's rubber boots and agreed. The farmer backed up, got a good running start, and kicked the lawyer in the groin with all his strength. Whitmore dropped to the ground and for 15 minutes rolled around in agony. Finally, in a tortured voice he growled, "Now, it's my turn!"

"Nope!" said the farmer. "Keep it. I give up."

Carrillo, a Southern California magistrate, had just ruled on a case, and an attorney for the defense jumped to his feet and questioned the judge's decision.

"I can't reopen the case after I've given my decision," said Judge Carrillo.

The lawyer replied, "Well, I guess I may as well leave, your Honor. There's no use knocking my head against a stone wall."

"I agree," said the judge. "But I don't know anyone who could do it with less personal injury than yourself."

**Where there's a will,
prosperity is just around the corner.**

"Who's the best lawyer in town?"
"Tim Cochrane, when he's sober."
"And who's the second best lawyer in town?"
"Tim Cochrane, when he's drunk."

What do you get if you combine a lawyer with a Godfather?
A contract you can't understand.

JUDGE:	Have you ever been in trouble before?
DEFENDANT:	Your Honor, all I did was to rob my kid brother's bank.
D.A.:	Your Honor, the defendant forgot to explain that his kid brother was treasurer of the First National Bank.

A crochety old resident of Santa Rosa was bitten by a dog, and he contended that it was his neighbor's canine. The neighbor was brought to court and offered this defense:
"Your Honor, first of all let me tell you my dog wouldn't do such a thing. Second, he is blind and can't see to bite anyone. Third, even if he could see, he couldn't stumble over to bite anyone on account of his lameness. Fourth, he has no teeth. And fifth, my dog died six weeks ago. Lastly, I never had a dog."

During a cross-examination of the witness, the counsel asked, "Now tell the court your name."
"Truman," replied the witness.
"And your first name?"
"Harry."
"Harry Truman, eh?" remarked the attorney. "That's a fairly well-known name."
"It ought to be," he replied, "I've worked in this town for the past twenty-five years."

Mahler was a little concerned about his pending court case. He asked his lawyer, "How should I plead?"
"On your knees," said the attorney.

How many law students does it take to screw in a lightbulb?
Six. One to change it and five to file an environmental impact report.

Lemongella, a Las Vegas lawyer, was invited to speak to a class at Harvard Law School. After completing the lecture, the attorney concluded by saying, "May God help you become truly learned in this law."
The students shouted, "The same to you."

At the graduation exercises, Ross accepted his law degree and then proudly approached his parents to receive their warm congratulations. Ross placed his hand on his father's shoulder, and smiled broadly. "Pop, it's time for a change," said the new lawyer. "All your life you worked hard for me, now it's time for you to go out and work hard for yourself."

All the new young law students gathered for the first day's classes.
The law professor stared at them, wiped his glasses, and then spoke. "You are about to embark on a course of study that will try your souls. Some of you will make it, and some will crack. Some will go on to bigger and better things. Those who crack will be lawyers."

**A lawyer will sometimes stay up
all night just to break a widow's will.**

A merchant retained an attorney to defend him in a suit for damages brought by an employee. Unfortunately for the attorney, his client lost the suit by furnishing evidence on the witness stand that was favorable to the prosecution to the tune of ten thousand dollars.

The merchant, naturally indignant, said, "If I had a son born an idiot, I'd make him a lawyer."

"Your father seems to have been of another opinion," rejoined the lawyer.

In what way does a lawyer resemble a pelican?
In the size of his bill.

Kessler arrived before the Pearly Gates and was startled by his reception. As he strolled up to the gate, he was greeted by a fifty-piece orchestra. Two hundred little angels tossed rose petals in his path, and he was welcomed by St. Peter with open arms.

"By golly, I'm really surprised at this greeting," offered the lawyer.

"Well," replied St. Peter, "you're a very special person."

"I don't understand," said the attorney.

"Oh," explained St. Peter, "you're the oldest lawyer who has ever entered our gates. You're 174 years old."

"Wait a minute. I think you're a little mixed up there, St. Peter. I'm only forty-six."

"Oh, I'm afraid you don't understand. We don't go by chronological age. We count your years by the number of hours you've billed your clients."

Santa Claus, the tooth fairy, an honest lawyer and a drunk were walking down the street together when they simultaneously spotted a hundred-dollar bill. Who got it?

The drunk, of course because the other three are mythological creatures.

Giordano, an immigrant, was called to give evidence in a trial involving a shooting.

"Did you see the shot fired?" began the judge.

"I no see it, but I'm-a tellin' you I heard it."

"That is not satisfactory. Step down."

As the Italian turned to go, he laughed. When he was immediately rebuked by the magistrate, he replied, "Hey, you Honna, did you-a see me laugh?"

"No, but I heard you."

"Atsa no satisfactory."

How can you tell when a lawyer is lying?
His lips are moving.

Attorney Maude Siebold was called to try a lawsuit in a small, very sleepy South Carolina town. She finished her business and as she paid her hotel bill, she said to the manager, "I intend, if possible, to come to this town to end my days."

"Really," said the manager. "Ah'm glad that yawl like our little town so well."

"You misunderstand," said Miss Siebold. "I want to end my days here because it seems to me that after a woman had lived here awhile, death would be a welcome relief."

The county's brightest attorney left the banquet hall with a look of self satisfaction. One of his colleagues stopped him and said, "Congratulations, Warren."

"Thank you!very much!"

"Were you surprised when you got the nomination as president of the Bar Association?"

"I surely was. My acceptance speech nearly fell out of my hand."

**The person who said
"talk is cheap" never hired a lawyer.**

Ms. Ellsworth, a Buffalo attorney who was quite short, appeared in court as a witness. She was cross-examined by lawyer Logan, who was over six feet five inches tall. Logan asked the witness, "What is your position?"

"I'm a member of the bar."

"You're a lawyer?" mocked the giant counselor. "Why I could put you in my vest pocket!"

"You probably could," snapped Ms. Ellsworth, "but if you did, you'd have more law in your vest pocket than you ever had in your head."

PROBATE

The place where lawyers recline
while they are waiting to get the money.

Coker visited a seriously ill lawyer in a Harrisburg hospital. He found him sitting up in bed, frantically leafing through the Bible.

"What are you doing?" asked Coker.

"Looking for loopholes," replied the lawyer.

The lawsuit was in full swing. Elena and Carlos Huerta were suing a Los Angeles trucking company as a result of a traffic accident.

"Mrs. Huerta, you say the collision threw you and your husband across the street and that your husband suffered a fractured skull and a broken arm. Tell us what happened to you. Were you hurt in the fracas?"

"Not exactly. Actually, it was a little higher up."

The ultimate in legal bills was received by a Hollywood restaurant owner. His attorney sent him a bill for eighty dollars "for waking up in the middle of the night and thinking about your case."

Metzger was in need of legal advice. He presented his case to Widder and asked what the attorney's fee would be.

"Well," said the lawyer, "I charge twenty dollars for advising you to do exactly what the law permits. For advice about how you can safely do what the law forbids, my minimum fee is two hundred dollars."

LAWYER

A brilliant person who rescues your estate from your enemies and keeps it for himself.

Reverend Lindsey engaged the services of Jessop, counselor-at-law, and soon received a bill. The clergyman went to see the lawyer.

"Pardon me, but I've always understood that you members of the bar were not in the habit of charging men of the cloth for your services."

"Allow me to correct you," replied Jessop. "You look for your reward in the next world, but we lawyers have to get ours in this."

A newly qualified judge in Louisiana was trying his first criminal case. Crawford, the prisoner before him, had appeared in court before on a similar charge and at that time was acquitted.

"Well," said the judge, "according to these records I see you're in the same kind of trouble."

"Yassir," said Crawford, "the last time yawl was mah lawyer, 'member?"

"Yes, I remember. Where is your lawyer this time?"

"Well, yore Honor, ah ain't got no lawyer this time. This time ah'm gonna tell the truth."

Practice does not make a lawyer perfect, but enough of it will make him rich.

The plaintiff's attorney was questioning the witness:
"What is your occupation?"

"I'm a bricklayer," answered the witness.

"Ha! A mere bricklayer, eh?" sneered the lawyer. "What do you think your position is in society?"

"Well, mister, I realize being a bricklayer ain't the most distinguished occupation in the world, but I feel I've done better than my father."

"And what was your father?" snapped the attorney.

"A shyster lawyer!"

"And what do you do, sir?"

"I'm a criminal lawyer."

"Aren't they all!"

A lawyer was trying to persuade his friend to undergo psychoanalysis. "It's really helped me tremendously," he said. "I was arrogant, vain, overbearing."

His friend looked up. "That was *before* analysis?"

LAWYER: Do you know what a conscience is?
WITNESS: Sure I do.
LAWYER: What is it?
WITNESS: My parents wanted me to be
            a lawyer, but I've got a conscience.

O'Flaherty, addicted to imbibing freely and often, was arrested for selling home-distilled whiskey. His lawyer put him on the stand and asked the jurors to look very carefully at the defendant.

"Now, ladies and gentlemen of the jury," concluded the lawyer, "you've looked carefully at the defendant. Can you honestly believe that if he had a quart of whiskey he would sell it?"

He was acquitted.

The American Bar Association was holding its annual convention in Manhattan. Mahaffey, Kilgore and Burke decided to do some sightseeing and wound up at the Empire State Building. As they stepped out on the observation deck high above the city, they were greeted by a mild-mannered, bespectacled young man standing on the edge of the railing.

"Hello there!" he shouted. "Are you fellows all lawyers from the convention?"

"Yes," said Burke. "Better get down before you fall!"

"It's all right!" said the man. "you can't get hurt falling from up here."

"Is that so?" asked Mahaffey.

"They've got giant fans on the 80th floor. If you fall from here it triggers the fans and they blow you right back up here again, safe and sound."

"Never heard of anything like that!" said Kilgore.

"Watch!" said the man, falling back over the rail. They rushed to the edge and saw him reach the 80th floor, then there was a gigantic SWOOSH! and he was blown back up to the roof safely. "It's great fun!" he cried, "Try it!"

The lawyers climbed up on the railing, linked arms and jumped. Down they fell to the 80th floor, and nothing happened! Then the 70th floor, 60th, 30th, 10th, SPLAT!

Costello and Jordan, two police officers, viewed the mess on the sidewalk. "More lawyers?" said Costello.

"Yes," said Jordan, shaking his head. "That damn Superman really hates them!"

Scientific researchers have decided they want to use lawyers for laboratory experiments instead of rats. There are more of them and you don't get so emotionally attached.

SURGICAL SMILES

**When a patient is at death's door it's
the duty of the doctor to pull him through.**

Blayden was very sick. He called Doctor Simper's office to set up an appointment. The nurse told him, "The next time that the doctor can see you is two weeks from today."

"I could be dead by then," said Blayden.

"Well, that won't be a problem," said the nurse courteously. "Just have someone let us know and we'll cancel the appointment."

Doctor Duffin was examining a patient when his nurse called him into the adjoining room. "The man you just examined walked out of the office," she said, "had a heart attack and dropped dead in the hall. What should I do?"

The M.D. answered, "Turn him around so it looks like he was coming into the office."

"My doctor says I need a complete change."
"What're you going to do?"
"I'm changing my doctor.

PATIENT: Do you think raw oysters are healthy?
DOCTOR: I've never heard one complain.

Did you hear about the doctor who treated a man for yellow jaundice and then found out he was Chinese?

SIGN IN DOCTOR'S OFFICE

The doctor is very busy.
Have your symptoms ready.

After a very thorough examination the doctor took Phipps into his office and said, "You're fit as a fiddle. You'll live to be eighty."
"But I am eighty," said the patient.
"See, what did I tell you!" said the M.D.

Randell, the captain of the college football team, was developing a painfully sore throat a few days before an important game. He rushed over to see the school physician. The doctor's door was opened by his pretty young nurse.
"Is the doctor in?" asked Randell in a bronchial whisper.
"No," whispered the nurse, looking quickly up and down the hallway, "come on in."

**Americans spent billions
on medicine last year — which proves
that a lot of doctors are feeling no pain.**

Surgical Smiles

Dr. Briggingham became quite popular in the community when he was given a big write-up in the local paper.

The next night at a cocktail reception he was approached by a middle-aged woman. "Oh, Doctor, I guess you don't remember me," she gushed. "Twenty years ago you came to see me at home and told me to stay in bed until you called back again. But you never came back!"

"Oh, my goodness," said the M.D., "then what are you doing out of bed?"

Verna, an attractive secretary, had just come out from under the anesthetic after an operation for appendicitis. She looked up at the surgeon with a smile. "Oh, doctor," she asked, "will my scar show?"

"No," said the medico, "not if you're careful."

Purvis went to see his friend Swilling who had been in an accident. He found Swilling lying in a hospital bed, swathed in bandages.

"What on earth happened?"

"This morning I went to see my doctor because I had a little headache."

"How does that account for the condition you're in?"

"I was given an emergency abdominal operation by mistake. I was only there in the first place because I rolled off the stretcher as I was being put in the ambulance; I broke my leg and three ribs."

"Ambulance? For a headache?" asked Purvis.

"The doctor said I needed more fresh air and advised me to go horseback riding. So I went out and rented a horse. But the animal got frightened by a passing scooter, I fell off and sprained my ankle. And that's why I'm like this."

**You don't know how indebted you are
to medical science — until you get the bill!**

The worried husband phoned his physician at 3 a.m. "Doctor, would you rush over? I'm afraid my wife has appendicitis," he pleaded.

"Impossible," said the doctor reassuringly, "just give her some carbonated soda and she'll go back to sleep."

"But Doctor, I tell you this is serious. Please come over right away."

"Now look, Mr. Phillips, three years ago I operated on your wife. I took out her appendix. Have you ever heard of anyone having a second appendix?"

"Doctor, please! Have you ever heard of anyone having a second wife?"

PATIENT: Doc, it's two o'clock in the morning
and I can't sleep. It's the bill I owe you.
I can't pay it. It bothers me so much
that I can't sleep.
DOCTOR: Why did you have to tell me that?
Now I can't sleep.

"This is really hard to believe."

"What?"

"My doctor gave me three pills. The blue one is for before dinner. The red one is for after dinner and the yellow one *is* dinner."

Dr. Dawson opened his office for the first time on Tuesday. No patient showed up until Friday morning. When the man came into his office, Dawson wanted to impress him. The young doctor picked up his telephone and barked into it, "I've got so many patients coming today I won't be able to get to the hospital to perform that heart transplant operation until late this afternoon."

Dawson hung up the receiver and turned to his visitor. "Now what seems to be your trouble?" he asked.

"Nothing," said the man. "I just came over to hook up your telephone."

Dr. Langwell stopped at a Kalamazoo cocktail lounge every evening on the way home for his own special drink: a frozen almond daiquiri. This concoction was made with the standard ingredients plus some crushed almonds. All Langwell had to do was come through the door, and the bartender would toss all the makings into the blender.

One evening, the bartender had the drink half-prepared when he discovered he was out of almonds. He added crushed hickory nuts instead.

The M.D. took one sip and asked the bartender, "Is this an almond daiquiri?"

"No," he replied. "It's a hickory daiquiri, Doc."

Doctor Thornton had been getting many calls from Mrs. Nash for free advice. Finally he decided to put an end to them after her next call. A few days later she telephoned about a problem with one of her youngsters.

"He has this red rash on his skin," she said. "What should I do?"

"That depends," said Thornton. "Hold him up so I can get a better look at him."

A Dublin physician once submitted a bill that stated:
"For curing your husband till he died."

Dr. Allan's advice was short and to the point. "You'll have to have regular habits from now on."

The young man protested, "But, doctor, I do have a lot of regular habits."

"Oh?" the physician was emphatic. "How come I saw you with a beautiful redhead at four o'clock this morning?"

"That, doc," explained the worn-out Romeo, "is one of my regular habits."

**Never go to a doctor
whose office plants have died.**

"Doc, you're charging me fifty bucks and all you did was paint my throat?"

"What did you expect for fifty dollars, wallpaper?"

Dr. Rosenstein lived in the slums of New York. He loved his profession and was thoroughly dedicated to his patients. Many of them were poor first-generation immigrants, living in abject poverty. Late one night, his bell rang, a woman stood there, shivering in the cold. After listening to her he dressed quickly and hurried to her flat, climbing six flights of stairs. There he examined the woman's daughter, Karolina.

"You've got a very sick little girl there," he said. "You've got to watch over her constantly. Get this prescription filled and follow the instructions carefully."

As he started to leave, his eye took in the pitiful conditions under which the family lived. He made no mention of a fee and carefully slipped a twenty-dollar bill beneath the prescription.

When Rosenstein called the next afternoon, Karolina was much improved. "I guess you found the money I left," he said.

"Oh, yes," smiled the mother. "Such a wonderful thing you did, it was enough for us to call in a better doctor."

We paid our annual visit to the family doctor. It was over in no time at all.

"Cough," said the doctor when we walked in.

"Cough up," said the receptionist when we walked out.

"My doctor is supposed to be a specialist but I'm not sure in what area."

"What do you mean?"

"He can only treat me if I'm sick from the head up, or from the ankles down."

Surgical Smiles

Dr. Jobson just finished giving Bastoni a routine check-up and reported favorably on his general condition.

"Doctor, what are my chances of living another 50 years?"asked Bastoni.

"How old are you?" asked the physician.

"I'm forty."

"How much do you drink?"

"I don't," said the patient.

"How many packs of cigarettes do you smoke a day?"

"I don't touch tobacco," replied Bastoni.

"Do you make extravagant demands on yourself — fast driving, gambling, excessive sexual activity?"

"I live a very orderly life, I have no vices whatsoever."

"Then why do you want to live another fifty years?"

Did you hear about the Denver doctor who has an interesting approach to medicine?

You open your wallet and he says, "Ah!"

Donaldson, a small-town doctor, hoped to ease the usual difficulty of securing payment from his patients. He posted a sign in his waiting room:

> $50 for the First Visit.
> $30 for the Second Visit.
> $20 for all Subsequent Visits.

One evening Lampkin went to Donaldson's office for the first time, and read the sign carefully. He then spoke to the physician, "Well, Doctor, here I am again for the third visit."

Donaldson eyed Lampkin up and down then said, "You're looking just fine. Continue with the same treatment. That will be twenty dollars."

Most doctors are fair. They don't operate unless they need the money.

"Doctor, I just wanted to let you know that there is an invisible man in your waiting room."
"Tell him I can't see him now."

BUMPER STICKER

Doctors do it with patience.

Gordon and Chambly, two Seattle M.D.s, were sunbathing on the beach at Acapulco.
"What wonderful legs that girl has!" exclaimed Gordon.
"I really didn't notice," replied Chambly. "I'm a chest man myself."

SHAPELY SHOWGIRL:	I want you to vaccinate me where it won't show.
DOCTOR:	Okay, my fee is twenty dollars, in advance.
SHAPELY SHOWGIRL:	Why in advance?
DOCTOR:	Because I often weaken in such cases and don't charge anything.

A notorious middle-aged bachelor was told by his doctor to start leading a saner life or face an early grave.
The first week he cut out cigarettes, the next he cut out liquor and the third week he cut out women.
The fourth week he started to cut out paper dolls.

**Some doctors tell their patients
the worst — others mail the bill.**

78

Surgical Smiles

"Doctor, I'm telling you, there's something really wrong with my stomach."

"Keep your coat buttoned and nobody will notice it."

McAlpine was choking on a chicken bone. He hurriedly called for the doctor who removed it.

"What do I owe you?" asked McAlpine.

"At least half of what you were ready to pay when the bone was still in your throat," replied the physcian.

Dubrow, a middle-aged Baltimore businessman, went to visit Doctor Boland. He wanted advice on what he could do to live to be one hundred years old.

"Well," said Boland, "you'll have to give up smoking, drinking, and women."

"Gosh, will that make me live to be one hundred?" inquired Dubrow.

"No," said the M.D., "but it will make it seem like it."

"Jim, you'd better brace yourself," said the doctor to his patient. "I've got some bad news."

"What is it?" asked the slightly panicked young man.

The doctor said, "Jim, I hate to say it, but you've only got six months to live."

"Six months!" screamed the patient. "My goodness, what am I going to do?"

The doctor shrugged, "If I were you, I'd get married and move to Kansas. It'll be the longest six months of your life."

"You got a good doctor?" asked Pryor.

"I'll tell the world." said Knatz. "He's a really nice guy. When he treated me for double pneumonia he sent me a bill for only one pneumonia."

BARROW: If I let you operate can you promise
I'll be back playing the piano in two weeks?
DOCTOR: I can't promise the piano but the last
time I performed this type of operation
the patient was playing the harp in two days.

Did you hear about the new tranquilizer atomizer?
One spray and it calms you down to the point where you can take a pill.

After having lunch at a church social, Dr. Pendlebury took a stroll in the churchyard nearby. One of the other guests asked where he'd gone.

"Oh, he's just stepped out," smiled the vicar, "to visit some of his old patients."

Nurse Lowell reported to the doctor that her patient didn't think he was getting enough attention.

"Well, give him what he wants," suggested the doctor.

"I'll quit first."

Doc Brown's battered jalopy — a Ford Edsel to be precise — was the subject for considerable merriment for the younger fry in front of the village drug store.

Doc Brown ignored the jibes as he climbed into the seat, then remarked amiably, "This car's paid for boys. If you'll check with your parents, you'll discover that you ain't."

**Today, it isn't an apple that
keeps the doctor away — it's his fees.**

Surgical Smiles

Winslade, a surgeon, Dow, an internist and Strutt, a radiologist, were drinking in a bar. Each doctor was boasting about how smart his dog was.

Winslade whistled for his collie. The animal draped some dog biscuits with a napkin and made a neat surgical incision with a knife. The onlookers applauded politely.

"Okay," said Dow, "just watch what my fox terrier can do." The internist called his pooch. It proceeded to clean up the mess made by the surgeon's dog and then sorted the fragments of dog biscuit by size, neatly and analytically.

Everyone was amazed, except the radiologist. "Now see what a real doctor's dog can do." Strutt called his hound. It ran in, gobbled up all the dog biscuits and then took the rest of the afternoon off.

YOUNG DOCTOR:	I took my new car to be repaired and the garage man charged me $800.
OLD MEDICO:	That's outrageous!
YOUNG DOCTOR:	Well, you see, he didn't know what was wrong with it so he had to call for a consultation.

Berger visited Dr. Hodgeson. "Doc, I've got terrible neck pains, throbbing headaches, and dizzy spells."

After a thorough examination Hodgeson said, "I'm really sorry to have to tell you this but I'm afraid you've got only two months to live."

The doomed man decided to spend all his money and enjoy his remaining life. First, he'd get something he'd always wanted — a dozen tailor-made silk shirts. After measuring him the tailor said, "That's a size 17 neck."

"Hold on," said Berger. "I wear a size 15."

The tailor remeasured him, "You're definitely size 17."

"I'm a 15," insisted Berger. "I always wear a 15 and that's what I want."

"All right, sir," said the tailor, "but if you wear a 15 you'll have terrible neck pains, throbbing headaches, and dizzy spells."

"Doc, you've gotta do something for me. I snore so loudly that I wake myself up."

"In that case, sleep in another room."

ADVERTISEMENT IN MEDICAL JOURNAL

> Vacancies exist for two female physiotherapists, preferably with some experience. Varied work embracing inpatients and outpatients.

Willoughby, a young intern, was handling his first case. He followed the book directly in his examination: height, weight, blood pressure, blood count, and he had just inserted the thermometer for a temperature reading. Willoughby made all the required notes on his little pad, then turning to his patient said, "Now sit down. I want to ask you a few questions."

"All right," said the patient, "but don't you think you better take the thermometer out first?"

DOCTOR: Our tests show you're going to have twins.

GIRL: That's impossible, I never doubled dated in my life.

"Don't worry," said Dr. Burstall to the anxious new mother. "The baby'll be fine. Just remember to keep one end full and the other end dry."

**A doctor will never violate his oath —
the oath he took to become a millionaire.**

Surgical Smiles

Dunstan, a University of Miami medical student, read the first question in an examination: "Name five reasons why mother's milk is better for babies than cow's milk."

This was his answer: "First, because it is fresher; second, it is cleaner; third, the cats can't get it; fourth, it is easier to take to movies and picnics."

Then Dunstan thought for a moment and added, "Fifth, it comes in such a cute little container."

He passed.

DOCTOR: Did you tell that idiot med student boyfriend of yours my opinion of him?

DAUGHTER: Of course, Daddy.

DOCTOR: Good. And what did he have to say to that?

DAUGHTER: Nothing much. Just that your diagnosis was as bad as ever.

How many pre-med students does it take to screw in a lightbulb?

Three. One to stand on a stool to screw it in and two to kick the stool out from under him.

"My doctor told me that I had to give up smoking, women and liquor."

"Well?"

"Now I'm looking for another doctor."

After complaining of abdominal pains, Carolyn, a chic fashion model, was being examined by her doctor.

"Well, miss, there's no doubt about it," said the M.D. "You have acute appendicitis."

"Thank you, doctor," said the girl, "but I came here to be examined, not admired."

Larner became very depressed and went to the hospital for a complete checkup. He said to the examining doctor, "I look in the mirror, and I'm a mess. My jowls are sagging. I have blotches all over my face. My hair is falling out. I feel ugly. What is it?"

"I don't know what it is," said the M.D., "but your eyesight is certainly perfect."

Did you hear about the female patient who wanted her doctor's assurance that his new treatment would not affect her complexion?

He refused to make any rash promises.

Then there was the billionaire Kuwaiti prince who went into the private nursing home for a gallstones operation.

He had a different surgeon for every stone.

"I'm afraid, doctor," said Mrs. Goddard to her physician, "that my husband has some terrible mental affliction." She paused a moment and then continued. "Sometimes I talk to him for hours and then discover that he literally hasn't heard a word I said."

"That doesn't sound like an affliction," replied the M.D., "that's a divine gift."

A Duluth druggist filled a prescription, then handed his customer a little bottle with 12 pills in it, and said, "That'll be $10.50."

Suddenly the phone rang and as the druggist turned to answer it, the customer put 50 cents on the counter, and walked out. The druggist turned back and spotted the 50 cents. "Sir!" he shouted but the guy was gone.

The druggist picked up the half a buck, looked at it, shrugged, flipped it into the till and mumbled, "Oh, well, I guess 40 cents profit is better than nothing."

Surgical Smiles

Mrs. Kerr was sitting in the doctor's office when he came in and said, "Madam, this isn't a urine sample you brought in. It's apple juice."

"Oh, my heavens!" she exclaimed, "I must've packed the other bottle in Ludwig's lunch box."

NURSE: Turn over, it's time for your shot.
PATIENT: Does it make a difference which
            cheek it goes in?
NURSE: No. Which cheek would you like it in?
PATIENT: Yours!

One day at dinner, Feinstein said to his wife, "I have to admit I'm feeling much better since my operation, but I can't figure out why I got this big bump on my head."

"Oh, that," said his wife. "In the middle of your operation they suddenly ran out of ether."

Did you hear about the Detroit doctor who sent a patient a get-well card and inside was a bill for $3.29?

It was for the card and the postage.

"I do like your uniform," prattled the young charmer. "Tell me what you do exactly."

"I'm a naval surgeon, miss."

"Really," replied the young lady, wide-eyed. "How you doctors do specialize!"

**Many people call a doctor when
what they really want is an audience.**

85

Daigler went to see a psychiatrist. He said, "Doc, I got this terrible feeling that everybody's trying to take advantage of me."

"No need to be concerned, that's a very common fear," responded the analyst. "Everybody thinks that others are trying to take advantage of them."

"Boy, Doc, that's such a relief!" sighed Daigler. "How much do I owe you?"

"How much have you got?" answered the shrink.

How many shrinks does it take to screw in a light bulb?

Only one, but it will take a very long time and will be very expensive.

In Laramie, a bowlegged cowboy completed his physical. "Well, doc, how do I stand?" he asked.

"That's what I'd like to know," said the physician.

Groman visited Doctor Semler to complain of insomnia.

"Don't you sleep at all at night?" asked the medico.

"Oh, I sleep like a top at night," admitted Groman. "And I sleep fairly soundly during the mornings. But I often have difficulty dropping off in the afternoons."

Brenton was trying to describe his excruciating symptoms to an impatient physician. "It's sort of a jabbing pain in my right shoulder, doctor. I get it when I lean forward, stretch out one arm, then the other, raise my elbows, hunch my shoulders and then stand up straight."

"Is that so?" sneered the physician. "Did it ever occur to you that you could avoid this mysterious pain simply by not going through such an absurd series of movements?"

"It did occur to me, doc," said Brenton, "but I couldn't think of any other way of getting into my overcoat."

Surgical Smiles

Boyd and Hatcher, two psychiatrists, were having lunch. "Do you know how Yuppies wean their children?" asked Boyd.

"Not really," admitted Hatcher.

"They fire the maid."

The head surgeon of a large midwest hospital called Osgood, one of his aides, into the office. "I realize that someday I'm going to pass on," said the doctor. "I'd like you to find a nice burial place for me."

Two weeks later, Osgood returned and said, "I've found just the spot. It's on a hill overlooking a beautiful stream. And the sun hits it during the day almost as if you were being spotlighted."

"Sounds good," said the M.D. "How much?"

"Four hundred thousand dollars."

"Four hundred thousand dollars?" shouted the surgeon. "But I'm only gonna be there three days!"

FENTON: Doctor! I'm suffering from hallucinations.
DOCTOR: Nonsense! You're imagining things.

"Come, come," the smiling psychiatrist said to his sobbing patient. "You mustn't carry on like this. Cheer up! Be happy!"

"Be happy!" echoed the tearful woman. "How can I be happy? Sixteen children I've had by that husband of mine — and he doesn't even love me! What is there for me to be happy about?"

"Well," suggested the doctor, "imagine what it would have been like if he did love you?"

Overton, sitting in the dentist's chair, shouted, "Hey, Doc, you haven't pulled the right tooth!"

"I know it," replied the D.D.S., "but I'm coming to it."

87

"Excuse me, doctor but there's a man outside with a wooden leg named Cramden."

"What's the name of his other leg?"

"Doctor, my hair is coming out. What can you give me to keep it in?"

"How about a cigar box?"

Mrs. Dockendorf had been to see dozens of doctors all over the world and none of them could find the cause of her illness. One day while driving through a very run-down neighborhood in a seedy part of town she passed a delapidated building. On the outside hung a decaying medical emblem. She entered a reception room and found Dr. Pedlum seated there reading a racing form.

Mrs. Dockendorf told him every detail of her experiences. After an hour of listening Pedlum said, "Stick your tongue out."

She did.

"I'm afraid you have GOK," said the M.D.

"GOK? Are you sure?"

"The clearest case of GOK I ever saw."

"What medicine will I have to take?"

"No medicine, ma'am. There is no cure for GOK."

Pedlum then collected his fee of fifty dollars and showed her to the door.

That night his phone rang. It was Mrs. Dockendorf's son. "Doctor," he said, "I understand you diagnosed my mother's ailment as GOK."

"That's right!"

"What does that mean?"

"It's an abbreviation illness."

"I don't understand."

"GOK," said the M.D., "stands for 'God only knows.'"

POLITICAL PEARLS

**Politicians are divided
into three groups: The anointed,
the appointed, and the disappointed.**

The staunch Republican New Yorker complained to a friend, "The Democrats have made it tough for me to get out of New York City. I have to go out the Franklin D. Roosevelt Drive, past four Johnson restaurants to get to Kennedy Airport."

"Tell you what," said his Democratic buddy, "why not save up enough Lincoln pennies, buy a ticket to Hoover Dam — and jump off!"

**When politicians say they are
appealing to all the intelligent voters
they mean those who will vote for them.**

What's the difference between a statesman and a politician?

A statesman is a man who thinks he belongs to the state; a politician is a man who thinks the state belongs to him.

A lawyer, a senator, and a business executive were on a fact-finding mission when their plane crashed. They were captured by cannibals and the chief told them they could each have one last wish before they were placed in a big pot and boiled to death.

The lawyer said, "Chief, your excellency, I would like to present you with my business card."

The chief accepted the card.

The senator said, "I'd like to give my speech on the ten greatest accomplishments of my career in government."

The chief said, "Okay," then turned to the executive.

"My last wish," said the businessman, "is that you cook me first. I've heard that speech three times."

A recent governor of Kansas was greeting an endless line of constituents when suddenly one pest showed up who wouldn't let go of the governor's hand.

"Say," the pest demanded, "I'm willing to bet that you can't tell me my name."

"Of course, I can," lied the Republican governor, trying to pry his hand loose. "Why, you and me, we've been workin' together for the same things now for years."

"Sure, sure," cajoled the constituent, "but you just try and tell me my name."

The governor called over an aide. "For God's sake, find out this twerp's name and tell him what it is!" exclaimed the governor. "He's forgotten it and he's trying to find it out from me!"

Politics is not a bad profession. If you succeed there are many rewards. If you disgrace yourself or go to jail, you can always write a book.

Political Pearls

How many Republicans does it take to screw in a light bulb?

Three. One to change the bulb, and two to blame the Democrats for the one that burned out.

Coming home late one evening, Blake heard his daughter's voice through a closed door. "No, Raymond, I can't do it," she said.

"What would it matter?" countered a male voice.

"Perhaps you're right. But I'm telling you I can't," resisted the daughter.

"Look, honey, no one would ever know but you and me," urged Raymond.

"No, it's a question of family pride. I have to think of my family, and I won't do a thing like that."

"Please," pleaded the man. "You don't know how happy it would make me."

"Nothing doing. I'm going to vote the straight Democratic ticket just like my grandfather and my father, even if you are a Republican."

POLITICIAN

One who goes to great lengths to say nothing,
then complains when no one quotes him.

At a Washington cocktail party, Booke, a visitor to the capitol city, was introduced to a congressman. After a while Booke asked, "Tell me, sir, what do you consider the object of legislation?"

"The greatest good to the greatest number," replied the politician.

"And," the visitor persisted "what do you consider the greatest number?"

"Number One!" replied the congressman.

Members of opposite parties will always be fighting. It's part of politics. Once a Democratic congressman walked up to a Republican after hearing him speak and shouted, "You can just go to hell!"

"Thanks!" replied the Republican, "that's the first time I have ever been invited to Democratic headquarters!"

What's the difference between a cowboy and a politician?

The cowboy gets up early in the morning, decides what he wants to do, then straddles his pony and gets to work. He does the best he can and spends as little money as possible.

The politician gets up late in the morning, straddles the fence, spends all the money he can, gets all the votes lined up, and then decides what to do.

"Are you going abroad next summer?" asked the Republican constituent of his congressman.

"No," he replied. "What's the use of traveling around among people who don't speak my language and who couldn't vote for me even if they did?"

"All right, what's on the agenda today?" someone asked at a big state meeting of the Democratic steering committee. "Anybody know?"

"Yeah," replied a staunch party member. "It's to determine whether we should have a convention to nominate delegates who will be voted on as to whether they will attend a caucus which will decide whether we should have a primary to determine whether the people will have to vote on this same question again next year."

There are two sides to every question — and a good politician takes both.

Political Pearls

How many Democrats does it take to screw in a light bulb?

Thirty. One representative from every socio-economic group.

A senator, a clergyman and a Boy Scout were passengers in a small plane that developed engine trouble.

"We'll have to bail out," the pilot announced. "Unfortunately, there are only three parachutes. I have a wife and seven small children. My family needs me. I'm taking one of the parachutes." And he jumped.

"I'm the smartest politician in the world," said the senator. "The country needs me; I'm taking one of the parachutes." And he jumped.

"I've had a good life," said the clergyman to the Boy Scout. "Yours is still ahead of you. You take the last one."

"Don't need to," shrugged the youth. "There are two parachutes left. The smartest politician in the world jumped with my knapsack."

How do you put a twinkle in a presidential candidate's eye?

Shine a flashlight through his ears.

"Our files are so crowded," said the chief clerk to the bureau head in congressional communications, "that we have to destroy all correspondence more than six years old."

"It's all right. Go ahead and do it," said his bureaucratic boss. "But first be sure to make copies of everything marked for destruction."

The trouble is there are too many Democrat and Republican senators and not enough United States senators.

93

A politician never burdens anyone with his troubles. Half the folks aren't the least bit interested, and the rest are delighted that he's getting what they think is coming to him.

Mrs. Green had gone into politics, and for months she was out of the house most of every day.

One night she returned at ten o'clock and sank into an armchair. "Everything's grand," she said. "We're going to sweep the country."

"That's very good, dear," said her husband, "Why not start with the kitchen?"

What did the presidential candidate say when his wife blew in his ear?

"Thanks for the refill."

A Westchester GOP committeewoman returned from New York to party headquarters disheveled and distraught.

"What happened?" asked a fellow Republican woman.

"I was in the garment district at the same time the Democrats were holding a rally. The mobs were thick and disorderly. Then, two muggers grabbed me and pulled me into an alley, tore off my clothes and jewelry and stole my purse. It was horrible."

"Didn't you scream?" asked the Republican co-worker.

"What, and have those damned Democrats think I was cheering for them?"

What's the biggest difference between the Iraqis, the Iranians, and the Americans?

The Iraqis shoot their mistakes, the Iranians repeat them, and the Americans reelect them.

Honesty is the best policy, but not the best politics.

94

Political Pearls

When an airplane carrying Chicago's long-time Mayor Richard Daley, Ferdinand Marcos and Richard Nixon suddenly developed engine trouble over the Pacific, a decision had to be made as to who would get the only available parachute. Marcos suggested it be put to a democratic vote.

Mayor Daley won, 15-2.

POLITICIAN

The guy who is always ready
to lay down your life for his country.

How many bureaucrats does it take to screw in a light bulb?

One, but he'll need two outside consultants.

A Latin American dictator stood up before a crowd and demanded, "Who should be your president?"

"You should be president!" came the roared reply.

"And for how long should I be president?"

"President for life!" they yelled in response.

"And what should I be paid?"

"Everything we have!" shouted the crowd.

"Good!" said the dictator. "I accept. Everyone who has voted may lower his hand and step away from the wall."

"Did your paper say that I was a liar and a scoundrel?"

"No sir," offered the city editor. "It must have been the *Times*. We never print stale news."

He was the busiest politician in Washington. He spent half his time passing laws, and the other half trying to help his friends get around them.

A good Republican knows how to say nothing. He just doesn't always know when. He can talk for an hour without mentioning what he was talking about.

Sometimes you wonder if anything will ever be done to reduce the size of the government bureaucracy. Some years ago a congressman offered an amendment to the farm bill to ensure that "the total number of employees in the Department of Agriculture at no time exceeds the number of farmers in America."

It lost: 230-171.

With her son in prison, Mrs. Gwynne decided to turn to the local politician for help. "My innocent son is in jail and I want you to get him released," she cried. "We voted and campaigned for you and now it's your turn to help us out."

"Don't worry," said the politico, "I'll help your boy. With my influence I can't fail."

A week later Mrs. Gwynne read the paper and spotted her son's picture with a number across his chest. She phoned the politician and screamed, "You and your influence. Did you see his picture in the paper tonight?"

"Yes, but did you notice the nice low number I got him?"

How many Washington bureaucrats does it take to screw in a light bulb?

One to spot the burned-out bulb, his supervisor to authorize a requisition, a requisition typist, twelve file clerks to file requisition copies, a mail clerk to deliver the requisition to the purchasing department, a purchasing agent to order the bulb, a clerk to forward the purchasing order, a clerk to mail order, a receiving clerk to receive the bulb.

Politics make strange bedfellows. That's how learning to sleep with one eye open was invented.

Political Pearls

A New England congressman was recently defeated in his fight for reelection. He inserted the following ad in his local newspaper:

> I wish to thank all of those who voted for me, and my wife wishes to thank all those who didn't.

No politician ever really believes what he says — that's why he is always amazed when you do.

A politician planned to run for office and wanted to know how he stood with the public, so he hired a pollster. A week later he received a report.

"Well," asked the politico, "what's the scoop?"

"Ninety eight percent of the people are for you. Funny thing is, I only kept running into the other two percent."

DAN: I hear you applied for a government job. What are you doing now?

TOD: Nothing. I got the job.

In ancient Greece, in order to prevent idiot statesmen from passing stupid laws upon the people, a practical solution was instituted. Lawmakers were asked to introduce all new laws while standing on a platform with a rope around their neck. If the law passed the rope was removed. If it failed, the platform was removed.

The reason a politician stands on his record is to keep the public from examining it.

You take a Democrat and a Republican and keep them both out of office, and they'd probably both make good citizens.

—WILL ROGERS

A politician made a fervent campaign speech in the Brownsville section of New York City for Abe Bierman, who was running for assemblyman.

"For every letter in the alphabet," shouted the orator, "Bierman has a virtue. Then he started counting off on his fingers. "A: he is able. B: he is brave. C: he is courageous. D: he is daring. E: he is efficient. F: he is frank. G: he's great. H: he's honest. I: he's intelligent ..."

One of the spectators in the front, who had been a long personal foe of Bierman's, jumped to his feet, pushed the politician into the background, and cried: "I will finish this list — J: he is a jerk. K: he is a kook. L: he is a louse. M: he is a murderer. N: he is a no-good. O: he is odious. P: he is a punk. Q: he is queer. R: he is a rat. S: he stinks. T: he is a thief. U: he is undependable. V: he is a varmint. W: he is a waster, and XYZ: which rhymes with SOB."

At a Washington cocktail party two strangers struck up a conversation. After a few minutes of small talk one said, "Have you heard the latest White House joke?"

The second fellow held up his hand and said, "No, wait, before you begin, I think I should tell you that I work in the White House."

The first fellow replied, "Oh, don't you worry, I'll tell it very slowly."

You can fool some of the people all of the time, and all of the people some of the time, and the rest of the time somebody else will fool them.

Political Pearls

What do you call five presidential candidates standing side-by-side in a row?

A wind tunnel.

A candidate stood alone on the stage of an empty auditorium. The audience didn't show up, but he continued to make his speech anyhow. He shouted, "If I am elected, I will give the people higher wages and cheaper housing." Then he would swear at himself.

He continued, "If I'm elected, I will see that everybody has health care and affordable automobile insurance." Then he began swearing at himself again.

A passing policeman heard the man talking to himself, then swearing at himself and asked, "What are you doing?"

"With nobody here I'm speaking out loud, talking to myself, and as a candidate I'm promising all these things to the voters."

"It's okay if you want to talk to yourself and make those promises," replied the officer. "But why do you keep swearing at yourself after every statement?"

"'Cause I hate liars."

FIRST CITIZEN: It must be terrible for two great political leaders to split.

SECOND CITIZEN: Not if they split 50-50.

When Vice President Dan Quayle was introduced to Mikhail Gorbachev, he noticed the former Soviet leader's red blotched skin.

"What is that mark on your head?"

"That's a birthmark!" answered Gorbachev.

"How long have you had it?"

**To err is human. To blame it
on the other guy is politics.**

99

"Are you a politician?" the kid asked the department store Santa Claus.

"Why do you ask?" ho-ho'd the jolly old elf.

"Because you always promise more than you deliver."

What's the difference between baseball and politics?
In baseball, if you get caught stealing, you're out!

"Senator, how do you answer the allegations against you of greed and corruption in office?"

"That's easy! I denounce the allegations and I denounce the alligators."

McDermot, the Democratic ward boss, was approached by Popkin, a wealthy neighborhood businessman who needed some favors.

The tycoon offered McDermot a new sports car, but the wily politician declined.

"My deep sense of public service," he explained, "and innate honesty prevents me from accepting."

"Okay," said Popkin. "How about if I sell the car to you for $10?"

"Well, in that case," said McDermot, "I'll take two."

After giving what he considered a stirring, fact-filled campaign speech, the candidate looked out at his audience and confidently asked, "Now, are there any questions?"

"Yes," came a thundering voice from the rear. "Who else is running?"

**Some politicians change sides
more often than a windshield wiper.**

Political Pearls

When Mrs. Eisenhower went abroad after her husband's death, she feared there would be unnecessary fuss made over the wife of a former President.

"Don't worry," said the friend with whom she was traveling. "In the little places where we'll be stopping most of the people don't know one president of the United States from another. I'm sure no one will bother you."

And no one did. But in Rome they received word that reservations for them had been made in a small Italian town.

When they reached the hotel in question they were received pompously by the manager. "We are proud to welcome the wife of the great President of the United States," he said, bowing. "Will you register, Mrs. Lincoln?"

GOVERNOR: (*On visit to factory*) Hello there, my good man.
WORKER: Forgotten my name, have you? Don't you remember me from your home town?
GOVERNOR: I remember your name very well, but I've completely forgotten your face.

Eleanor Roosevelt had many qualities that were truly beautiful. But she was not a physically attractive woman. This was a story she loved to tell on herself.

Late one night she got on a train in Washington bound for New York where she was scheduled to give a speech. It was tough to get space on a train during the war, but they stopped the train. Mrs. Roosevelt got on and went directly to her lower berth. She tried to get to sleep but a man in the upper berth kept snoring. His loud snoring became so unbearable that Mrs. Roosevelt began jabbing the guy with her umbrella.

Finally, he woke up and said, "It won't do you no good lady, I had a good look at you when you got on the train."

**What any government needs
is more pruning and less grafting.**

A young political candidate once asked Mark Twain for advice. Twain offered counsel by telling him of a farmer who aspired to serve in the Missouri state legislature.

"This farmer was anxious to make a good impression and thought he could do this by using every big word he could find in the dictionary," related the great humorist. "As a result, his speeches were almost impossible to follow and his campaign made little progress."

"What happened?"

"One evening the candidate was milking a cow and practicing one of his speeches at the same time. The cow, evidently fed up with his harangue, kicked him in the jaw, causing him to bite off the end of his tongue."

"Well," commented the young candidate, "I suppose that put an end to his career as a politician."

"Oh, no," replied Twain. "After that he could use only words of one syllable, and it made his speeches so simple and appealing to the farmers he was reelected every time."

Lyndon B. Johnson was a feisty, colorful character known for his rough language, especially when he was the Senate Minority Leader.

One day Johnson was not in the Senate when a vote was taken on an important issue. The Republicans won because a Democrat had switched his vote.

Later the switch senator asked a colleague what Johnson had said about his vote. "Do you want me to leave out the swear words?"

"Yes, of course."

"Then, he didn't say anything."

Another time when Majority Leader Johnson was limping around the office with a sore toe, an aide passed along this gem: "LBJ went for a walk last night and was hit by a motor boat."

**Every politician wants to
make a name for himself. Most of these
names can't be printed in a family newspaper.**

Political Pearls

The only persons not allowed to hold elected office are lunatics and convicted felons. Law-abiding Americans always thought it was the other way around.

STATESMAN

A politician who never got caught.

On election day in Georgia a man walked up to a farmer as he came out of a voting booth and said, "Excuse me, sir, I'm from the FBI."

"Howdy, young fella," said the farmer. "What seems to be the trouble?"

"We happen to know that you accepted a sizable bribe and you sold your vote."

"'T'snt true. Ah only voted for the candidate because Ah like him."

"I'm afraid, that's where we've got you. We have concrete evidence you accepted fifty dollars from him."

"Well, it's plain common sense, if someone gives you fifty dollars, you're gonna like him."

YOUNG WOMAN: *(About to attend Republican rally)* I'm not prejudiced at all. I'm going to listen to that bunch of crap with a perfectly open and unbiased mind.

How many bureaucrats does it take to screw in a light bulb?

None. "We contract out for things like that."

In crime, the theory is take the money and run. In politics, it's run — and then take the money.

I can still remember the first time I heard Hubert Humphrey talk. He was in the second hour of a five-minute speech.

— GERALD FORD

How many bureaucrats does it take to screw in a light bulb?

Two. One to assure us that everything possible is being done while the other screws the bulb into a water faucet.

Did you hear about the new bill that will solve the problem of political graft?

If passed, it will make all bribes to public officials taxable.

Culbreth, Moore and Tayback, three prominent surgeons, were drinking together and swapping stories in the bar of the Desert Springs Marriott.

"You know," said Culbreth, "a guy lost an arm and I gave him a new one. Within a month he was out looking for work."

"So what?" retorted Moore. "I gave a fella a heart transplant and within two weeks he was looking for work."

"That's nothing," said Dr. Tayback. "We transplanted a whole person from Washington D.C. and pretty soon everyone all over the country was looking for work."

A couple was leaving a party at the White House. The woman said, "I'd like to say goodbye to the President."

Her husband said, "Who wouldn't?"

Some people think our President should be limited to one six-year term. Actually, all politicians should be given six-year terms with possible time off for good behavior.

Political Pearls

Adlai Stevenson did a great job as Attorney General of Illinois. He arranged for the cops in Chicago to wear striped uniforms, so when they went to jail they wouldn't have to change.

— EVERETT DIRKSEN

This is a tale Harry Truman used to tell on himself and truly reflects the former President's sense of humor:

After Truman left the White House he went to visit an old friend who lived on Lake Shore Drive in Chicago. By mistake Truman rang the wrong doorbell and then apologized to the man who answered. The man accepted the apology, then looked at the former President and exclaimed, "Say, anybody ever tell you you're a spittin' image of that old SOB Harry Truman?"

Harry Truman had a little sign on his desk which expressed his feelings about the presidency. It read: *Always do right. This will gratify some people and astonish the rest.*

How many presidential candidates does it take to screw in a lightbulb?

One. He holds the lightbulb up to the socket and waits for the world to revolve around him.

Did you hear they're building an archive for the Nixon papers?

No admission charge — you have to break in.

One of Dan Quayle's aides walked up to him in the White House and said, "Mr. Vice President, the people want to know what we're going to do about the trade bill."

Quayle said, "I don't have that file with me but you can tell the people that if we owe it we're gonna pay it."

President Bush's plan for full employment is nearly complete. As of today, nearly everyone in his family is working. Statistics also show that not a single millionaire is looking for work.

Do most Americans approve of the way George Bush has handled the budget?

They've never been so indebted.

President Bush was bitten by a tsetse fly in Africa and was in a coma for three years. He awakened to find Vice President Quayle at his bedside.

"Easy, Mr. President," said Quayle, "I've been running the country during your illness and we are doing very well."

"How well?"

"I have the figures here," began Quayle, "but first, know that most of the countries in the world now have a democratic form of government. We only compete now on economic grounds. Inflation ran half of one percent last year and should be lower this year. Unemployment is holding steady at 2 percent and we have reduced the national debt by just over $100 billion."

"Incredible!" said the President, "I was right about you all along! Tell me about the cost of living. What does the average American family of four spend each week on food?"

"Not too much," said the Veep, "I would say about 5,000 yen."

CLERGY CLASSICS

**A clergyman is a man whose
mother practices what he preaches.**

Lintott invited his long time friend Gillespie to attend
Sunday services. On their way home Lintott asked, "How
did you like the minister's sermon?"

"To tell you the truth," replied Gillespie, "I like our own
minister better."

"Why is that?"

"It's the words they use," explained Gillespie. "Our
minister says 'In conclusion' and then he concludes. Your
minister says, 'Lastly,' and he lasts."

The best test of a sermon is depth — not length.

Old Mrs. Rotholz got into an argument with her pastor. The clergyman thought he would never see her again. However, she showed up for the evening service that very same Sunday.

"I thought you'd gone for good," he said to her.

"Pastor," she said, "I'm going to be loyal to my church, even if the Devil is in the pulpit."

PASTOR: Isn't this a beautiful church? Here is a plaque for the men who died in the service.
STAPLES: Which one? Morning or evening?

Pastor Beaven was approached one Sunday after the service by Chittel, a member of the congregation.

"Pastor," said Chittel, "you have a marvelous gift of oratory. How did you develop it?"

"I learned to speak as men learn to skate or ride a bike," answered the clergyman, "by doggedly making a fool of myself until I got used to it."

The Quades purchased a farm that was badly run down. The fields were overgrown with tall weeds, the woods uncleared and the buildings were falling apart.

Quade spent long hours every day for months trying to put it back into shape.

One morning Reverend Whitehead, who had been watching his work, stopped by to compliment him.

"It's wonderful the progress you and the Lord have made," said the clergyman.

"Yeah," said Quade, "but you should've seen this place when the Lord was working it alone."

**One reason we have so many
pennies in the church collection
plate is because we have no smaller coin.**

Clergy Classics

The new preacher, at his first service, had a pitcher of water and a glass on the pulpit. As he preached he drank until the pitcher of water was completely gone.

After the service someone asked an old woman of the church, "How did you like the new pastor?"

"Fine," she said, "but he's the first windmill I ever saw that was run by water."

CLERGY

Religious persons who decided to
go into their Father's business.

Western Union officials claim this actually happened in the spring of 1899:

Deacon Shipsley went to Omaha to purchase a new sign to be hung in front of his church. He copied the motto and dimensions, but when he got to Omaha he discovered he had left the drawing behind. He quickly wired his wife, "Send motto and dimensions."

An hour late, Miss Balsam, the new clerk who knew nothing of the previous message, returned from lunch. When the message came over the wire, she read it and fainted: "Unto Us A Child Is Born. 6 feet long, 2 feet wide."

A minister gave his teenage daughter a pedigreed puppy for her birthday, warning her that the little dog had not yet been housebroken.

Sure enough, an hour later when he wandered into his daughter's room, he found her contemplating a small puddle in the center of the room.

"My pup," she murmured sadly, "runneth over."

**A clergyman with no
politics is never made a bishop.**

Preacher Pankey aspired to public office. He stood up in the town square, exhorting the people to help him win the election. Then, like all preachers, he asked for a collection.

Pankey handed his hat down and asked that it be passed around. When the hat had gone through the crowd it arrived back at the platform without a single penny in it. The preacher looked into the black emptiness of the hat and raised his hands in pious fervor.

"Anyway, dear Lord," he cried, "let us be thankful that this hat got back safely through this crowd."

St. Patrick's Cathedral is being remodeled. They're going to install drive-in confessionals. It's called:
TOOT AND TELL.

Reverend Crombie and his shrewish wife were taking an evening stroll and turned down a rather shabby street. As they passed a large old house, three well-endowed and over-dressed young women all nodded and said, "Good evening, Reverend."

When the hookers were out of earshot, his wife asked, "Who are they?"

"Just some young women I know professionally," answered the red-faced minister.

"Their profession or yours?" asked the suspicious wife.

An agent with the Internal Revenue Service visited Reverend Campling. "Reverend," said the agent, "one of your parishioners, a Mr. K.L. Whorley, has claimed on his tax return that he made a two-thousand-dollar contribution to your church. Do you know if that's true?"

"Don't worry," said the minister, "if he didn't, he will."

To play a harp like an angel,
you've got to practice like the devil.

One summer the Baptists and Methodists agreed to stage an evangelical revival week. The Presbyterians reluctantly agreed to go along with it. At the end of the week the ministers got together to discuss the results of the session.

The Methodist said, "We won four new members."

Said the Baptist, "We did even better. Six people became converts to the Baptist faith."

They both turned to the Presbyterian and asked him how he did. "We did the best of all," answered the parson. "We didn't add any but we got rid of ten."

God's plan made a hopeful beginning,
But man spoiled his chances by sinning;
    We trust that the story
    Will end in God's glory,
But at present, the other side's winning.

An Arkansas congregation was about to erect a new church edifice. The building committee, after twelve consecutive meetings, passed the following resolutions:

(1) We shall build a new church.

(2) The new building is to be located on the site of the old one.

(3) The material in the old building will be used in the new one.

(4) We shall continue to use the old building until the new one is completed.

The women's auxiliary of the Evangelical Baptist Church were in favor of installing a new chandelier. A church conference was scheduled to discuss the matter.

Old Deacon Clodmoor, representing a faction that opposed this proposal, said, "We are against this here chandelier proposition for three reasons. In the first place, we can't even order one — nobody knows how to spell it! Second, there ain't nobody in our congregation that could play it. And third, what this church needs is more light!"

In Sunday school, little Muriel was asked, "Can you repeat a verse from the Bible that we studied last week?"

She replied, "Not only can I quote the verse, but I can also give you the zip code: Exodus: 19:20."

A six-year-old's version of the 23rd Psalm:
"He leadeth me beside distilled water."

During a test in confirmation class at a midwest Episcopal Church the children turned in these answers:

— It is often difficult to hear in church because the agnostics are so terrible.

— Lot's wife was a pillar of salt by day and a ball of fire by night.

— When Mary heard that she was the mother of Jesus she sang the Magna Carta.

—The fifth commandment is humor thy father and thy mother.

— Holy Acrimony is another name for marriage.

— Christians have only one wife; that is called "monotony."

TEACHER: In our lesson today we have talked about the burnt offerings offered in the Old Testament. Why don't we have burnt offerings today?

STUDENT: On account of air pollution.

Did you hear about the Hollywood actor who wrote a book on atheism and then prayed to God that it would be a bestseller?

The Sunday school question was, "Where is hell?" Almost instantly, little Stephanie's hand went up. "I think we have some of it," she said, "at home in our bathroom."

"Whatever makes you say that?" asked the teacher.

"Because whenever one of us is in there when Daddy wants to shave, he yells, 'Get the hell out of there'!"

SMALL BOY: Why don't you come to my church?
OTHER SMALL BOY: 'Cause I belong to another abomination!

Mrs. Lucas took little Teddy to a department store and bought him a new suit.

"Won't I look neat at Sunday school in this?" said the boy to his mother.

"Oh, do you go to Sunday school?" asked the clerk, as he wrapped the suit."

"Of course I do," Teddy said, "where else is there to go on Sunday?"

At Sunday school the clergyman concluded a story and said, "Now children, are there any questions?"

Andy raised his hand and asked pointedly, "Yes, how do you get into your collar?"

Pastor Fullerton, recovering from surgery, received a hand-written card from the kids in his Sunday school. He read it with mixed feelings:

"Dear Pastor, Get well soon. Rest in peace."

Miss Murphy was teaching the 23rd Psalm to her a Sunday school class .As the little voices chorused out, she seemed somewhere to detect a false note. She heard each of the children one by one, until at last she came across little Alex who ended with the following words: "Surely, good Miss Murphy shall follow me all the days of my life."

There was a young girl in the choir,
Whose voice went up hoir and hoir;
   Till one Sunday night
   It went out of sight,
And they found it next day in the spoir.

CHURCH SIGN

Come early. . . if you want a back seat.

Mrs. Wheatley listened to the bedtime prayer of her sleepy four-year-old daughter and was astonished to hear the child say:

Now I lay me down to sleep,
I pray the Lord my soul to keep;
And when he hollers let him go,
Eenie, meenie, miney, moe.

"Can any child give me a commandment with only four words in it?" asked the Sunday school teacher.
A little boy raised his hand immediately.
"You may answer, Gerald," said the teacher.
"Keep off the grass!"

One night, Driscoll, a bible salesman, was forced to stay in a small town. There was heavy rain and the roads were washed out.

He turned to the hotel coffee shop waitress and said, "This certainly looks like the Flood."

"The what?"

"The Flood. Surely you've read about the Flood and the Ark landing on Mount Ararat."

"No, mister, I'm 'fraid I haven't," she replied. "I ain't seen a newspaper for three weeks."

Mrs. Devlin was born in Boston and was raising her large family in that city. One day she went to confession and said to the priest, "I got 14 kids, don't you think it's time I took the pill?"

"You can't do that," he said, "that's against our religion. Have you tried the rhythm method?"

"Where in the world am I gonna get an orchestra at two o'clock in the morning?" she said.

Lynette was thinking of becoming a Catholic and asked a recent convert, "Tell me, does being a Catholic cut down on your sinning?"

"No," was the reply, "but it makes it more exciting."

A group of youngsters was caught with the evidence on them. All except Billy had sticky faces from the candy they had taken from a Milwaukee mall.

The policeman asked him, "How come you're not eating any? Didn't you help steal it?"

"Yes," said Billy. "I helped steal it but I didn't eat any of it. I gave mine up for Lent."

"And what did you give up for Lent?" asked little Ricky's aunt.

"I gave up ice cream!" he said. "All except chocolate."

Did you hear about the extremely religious moth who gave up woolens for lint?

Shortly after Pastor Pommer announced the birth of a son, the trustees of the church granted his request for an increase in salary.

This routine continued for several years. Each time a child arrived at the pastor's house, the church granted his request for a pay raise.

But a recession brought hard times and collections were sparse. So when Pommer announced the birth of another child the church elders firmly turned down his bid for more money. They scolded him for siring such a large family.

"You'll just have to get along on your present earnings," said Elder Bowerbank. "That's the way it will have to be."

The pastor replied, "May I remind you that it is the Good Lord who sends us children?"

"Quite right," said Bowerbank, "and the Good Lord also sends us stormy weather. But that's no reason why you shouldn't wear rubbers!"

Adam was extremely lucky. He didn't have to listen to Eve talking about the man she could have married.

MILITANT FEMINST

An adamant Eve.

Little Millie's mom asked her, "What did you learn today at Sunday school about the creation of Adam and Eve?"

"The teacher told us how God made the first man and the first woman," answered the child. "He made the man first. But the man was very lonely with nobody to talk to him. So God put the man to sleep, and while he was asleep, God took out his brains and made a woman of them."

The first man and woman were having their first argument. It concerned Adam's habit of going out at night. Eve was upset over his "berry-picking" jaunts. "Adam, do you have to stay out late every night?"

"That's silly," replied Adam. "You're the only girl for me. In fact, you're the only girl in the world."

That night when Adam fell asleep, he woke when he felt a poke in his stomach. "Eve, what are you doing?"

"Just counting your ribs."

Conversation between Adam
and Eve must have been difficult at
times because they had nobody to talk about.

At a Sunday school picnic Reverend Hanford was seized with a fit of sneezing while walking across a small footbridge. His false teeth flew from his mouth and landed in the clear water in the middle of the stream.

The minister was about to remove his shoes and wade in after them when old Mrs. Melson appeared on the scene, carrying a well-filled dinner basket.

When the elderly woman discovered the clergyman's plight, she reached in her basket and removed a crisp brown chicken leg, tied a string to it and tossed it into the water near the dentures.

Quickly the teeth clamped into the chicken leg and they were safely reeled in.

Did you hear about the Poughkeepsie parish that raises money with Bingo games? They have a sign in front of their church that reads:
LET US KNEEL AND PLAY.

Virtue is its own reward,
and a clergyman's income proves it.

A Chicago church ran raffles. Once a year they got three cars, parked them in front of the church, and sold chances on them. Each year they raffled off a Cadillac, a Buick and a Chevrolet.

Three days after one such raffle, Father O'Banion was walking down the street when he bumped into Hogarty coming out of a tavern. "Can you tell me who won the cars?" asked Hogarty. "Who won the Cadillac?"

"The Cardinal did," said the priest. "Wasn't he lucky?"

"Who won the Buick?"

"The monsignor did. Wasn't he lucky?"

"Well, who won the Chevy?" asked Hogarty.

"Father Kilkelly. Wasn't he lucky?" said the priest.

At that moment Hogarty started back into the saloon for another drink. The priest grabbed him and said, "By the way, how many tickets did you buy?"

"Not a damn one," said Hogarty. "Wasn't I lucky?"

Some churches will never admit it but there were actually 11 Commandments. The 11th was:
THOU SHALT NOT YELL "BINGO!"

Sharkey died and went to heaven. At six o'clock in the morning, they put him to work shining the Pearly Gates, polishing the stars, cleaning up all around heaven. He had to work until six o'clock that night. After several days of back-breaking labor he could stand it no longer and asked if he could take a rest. Sharkey got two days off.

He decided to visit purgatory and see what it was like down there. He wanted to know if they worked as hard as he did in heaven. Sharkey arrived at purgatory at nine o'clock in the morning, and everybody was just sitting around doing nothing.

"I don't get it," he said to an attendant. "I'm up in heaven and they work me steady from six in the morning till six at night every day. Down here where things are supposed to be so much tougher, you're all sitting around at nine in the morning doing nothing."

"It's easy to explain," said the attendant, "there are more of us down here, so we get finished sooner."

118

Clergy Classics

A West Virginia evangelist was speaking in a meeting when a heckler shouted, "Listen to him! And his father used to drive a wagon led by a jackass."

"That's right," said the evangelist, "and today my father and the wagon are gone. But I see we still have the jackass with us."

TEACHER: What is your favorite Bible story?
JUSTINE: Jesus at the wedding, changing water into wine.
TEACHER: What do we learn from this miracle?
JUSTINE: When you have a wedding, it's a good idea to have Jesus there, too.

When little Oswald was filling out the private boys' school questionnaire, he came to "Religion." After thinking about it for a while, he wrote "Jew."

When the director noticed the entry, he called the boy into his office. "Oswald," he said, "why did you write 'Jew' under 'Religion'? Don't you know you're an Episcopalian?"

"Of course I do," replied Oswald. "But I just couldn't spell Episcopalian."

Reverend Twickingham had gone to see an elderly parishioner and she presented him with a jar of peaches saturated in brandy. The minister opened the jar, took a whiff, and said, "Oh, my! You don't know how grateful I am for this."

"Really?" said the old lady. "It's only a small present."

"Yes, but it's not the present that counts," said the clergyman, "it's the spirit in which it's given."

**The best of ministers seldom preach,
but the best of preachers often minister.**

119

Graham dreamed that he had died and awakened in a vast expanse where he was exceedingly comfortable. He rested, then became bored and shouted, "Is anybody here?"

In a moment, a white-robed attendant appeared and asked, "What do you want?"

"What can I have?" asked Graham.

"You can have anything you want," replied the attendant.

"Well, bring me something to eat."

"What would you like to eat?" asked the attendant. "You can have anything you want."

Graham ordered a magnificent seven-course dinner. They brought him just what he wanted and he ate and slept and had a glorious time. He went on getting everything he wanted whenever he asked for it, but he became depressed and sent for the attendant.

"I'm bored," he complained. "I need something to do."

"I'm very sorry, but that is the only thing we cannot give you here."

"Well, I'm sick and tired of it. I'd rather go to Hell!"

"Where do you think you are?" exclaimed the attendant.

Hobson was delinquent in paying his pledge to the church and the matter was referred to Reverend Weames.

"You are a respectable citizen," chided the minister. "You always pay your debts to everyone else. Why not pay your debts to the Lord?"

"Tell you the truth," said Hobson, "He just doesn't push as hard as some of the others."

In a small village church old Mrs. Boggs, a poor widow, put $1 in the collection plate, twice her usual offering. The pastor asked, "Why?"

"My grandchildren are visiting," she replied.

Two weeks later Mrs. Boggs put a $5 bill in the plate and explained, "They just left."

If God were permissive, He
would have called them the Ten Suggestions.

Clergy Classics

Parson Heimer, from a little Louisiana church, developed a tick just above his right eye, which made him wink constantly. It got so bad he couldn't drive his car, so he boarded a bus for New Orleans to see an eye specialist.

As Heimer got on the bus, he asked the driver, "Will you find me a good taxi in town?"

The driver winked back and said, "Sure thing, buddy!"

When they pulled into the station, there were eight cabs waiting, but the driver tipped his cap, held up two fingers, and the next to the last taxi came rolling up. The preacher got in the cab and said, "Will you find me a nice hotel?"

The taxi driver winked and said, "Just leave it to me, buddy!" and headed off across town.

The hotel was small but elegant. The buxom desk clerk wore thick, heavy make-up. "What'll you have? Blonde, brunette or redhead?"

Almost too stunned to wink, the parson gasped, "But you don't understand! I'm not looking for a woman!"

Winking again, the clerk replied, "Now don't you feel bad, honey. Just sit right there and Sebastian will be right with you!"

CHURCH SIGN

This church is prayer conditioned.

Did you hear about the newest invention in collection boxes?

When you drop in a quarter or more it doesn't make a sound.

Drop in a dime and it tinkles like a bell.

A nickel blows a whistle, and a penny fires a shot.

And, when you don't drop in anything, the box takes your picture.

The Devil's traps are never set in the middle of God's road.

121

The minister told his congregation: "There is a certain man among us who is having an affair with another man's wife. Unless he puts ten dollars in the collection box, his name will be read from the pulpit."

When the collection box was emptied, there were nineteen ten-dollar bills plus a five and two singles clipped together with a note: "Other three payday."

Pastor Wadlow, in a new parish, wanted to know what the congregation thought of his preaching. He took the elderly sexton aside and asked him, "What do they say of Pastor Dodds, my predecessor?"

"Oh," said the sexton, "they say he's not sound."

"What do they say of the new minister?"

"Oh, they say he's all sound!"

One Sunday at a Toledo church, Forest walked out during the pulpit message. After the service, Reverend Pierpont asked his wife, "Was your husband ill?"

"No," she said, "he always walks in his sleep."

Stradling, a collector of rare books, was browsing at a Hartford garage sale when Holles struck up a conversation with him.

"I just threw away an old Bible that had been in our family for generations," said Holles. "Guten ... something printed it."

"Not Gutenberg?" gasped the book collector.

"Yes, that was the name."

"Good heavens, you've thrown away one of the first books ever printed. A copy recently sold at auction for $600,000."

"Mine wouldn't have been worth a dime," replied Holles. "Some clown by the name of Martin Luther had scribbled all over it."

Mrs. Hodge, age 73, on her way out of church, stopped beside her minister and said, "Thanks for the sermon, Reverend Pratt. I woke up from it refreshed."

Reverend Paulson stopped over for a night in a small Fresno motel. After dinner in the coffee shop there wasn't really anything for him to do. Finally he picked up the Gideon Bible that had been placed in the room. Pasted on the outside cover was a sticker that read: "If you are lonely and discouraged, read Psalms 23 and 27."

Paulson finished reading the two Psalms, then underneath the 27th Psalm, he saw a scribbled note that said: "If you're still lonely, call Linda 657-5872."

CHURCH SIGN

Come in and have your faith lifted.

Reverend Houseley preached all his life against the wickedness of betting. He was visiting Ireland and decided to attend a race to see for himself what went on.

At the track he saw a Catholic priest bless a horse about to run in a race. Houseley remembered the number of the horse, which won the race. He continued to watch the priest and saw him bless two more horses — both won their races.

After seeing a horse for the fourth race being blessed, the minister rushed to the betting window and placed all his money on it. The race started but before long the horse began to stagger and finally fell over dead.

Distraught, Reverend Houseley sought out the priest and told him his unhappy experience.

"I'm very sorry," said the Catholic. "I guess you must be a Protestant!"

"Indeed I am," said the clergyman.

"Ah, then," said the priest, "you would not be know'n the difference 'tween a blessin' and givin' the last rites!"

Two men named Henry Carter lived in the same high rise in Houston. One was a corporate exec, the other a preacher.

One day executive Carter took off for a convention in South Africa. After a terribly long and tiring trip he finally reached his destination. Immediately he cabled his wife to report his safe arrival, but the cable was delivered to the wrong apartment.

The Rev. Mrs. Carter, whose husband had died a few days earlier, puzzled over the message. It read: *Arrived Safely. Heat Unbearable.*

Felton's cocker spaniel died. He missed him like a son. He felt the only comfort he could get would be to see that the dog had a burial ceremony as elaborate and as solemn as a human being. There was a Methodist church on his street and it was there he applied.

The minister said, "I am sorry, it would be blasphemy to bestow upon an animal the ritual we offer a human being. There is a synagogue two blocks down. Their attitude may be different."

The rabbi listened but was even more discouraging. "You must understand," he said, "that a dog is ritually unclean. I am afraid I could not lend this temple to such a ceremony. It may be different elsewhere. There is a Catholic church nearby, perhaps they would be willing to help you."

Father Rourke listened and shook his head. "I truly sympathize with you in your sorrow, but it cannot be done."

"Father, to show you how much this animal meant to me," said Felton, "I was prepared to donate ten thousand dollars to any house of worship that would have taken care of my little dog for me."

"My son," said the priest. "Perhaps I've completely misunderstood all the facts. Did I understand you to say that the dog was Catholic?"

MILITARY MERRIMENT

**A GI is a young soldier whose combat
training is perfect preparation for marriage.**

In preparation for Operation Desert Storm, Armstrong
and Page, two G.I.'s from Kentucky, were on a transport
sailing to the Persian Gulf. Standing on the deck, they gazed
out across the vast expanse of water.

"That's the most water Ah ever seen in my life," said
Armstrong. "Did you ever see so much water?"

"No, man," said Page, "and that's just the top of it."

In Saudi Arabia, an American officer was visiting a gun
battery. During his tour of inspection he addressed
Edmondson, a young G.I. "Do you know what you would
do if the first gunner got his head blown off?"

"Nothing sir," answered the soldier.

"Why nothing?" asked the nonplussed officer.

"Well, sir, ya see," he replied, "I'm the first gunner."

One morning during the Gulf War an Iraqi officer approached the American lines holding a white flag.

"Flag of truce," he shouted.

"What do the Iraqi soldiers want?" asked a sergeant.

"We would like to exchange a couple of generals for a can of condensed milk."

Saddam Hussein was being driven to Kuwait City when his armored limousine hit a donkey.

"We must show concern for peasants," Saddam told his driver. "Go to the house immediately and apologize for killing their mule!"

The driver obeyed and returned a few minutes later with his arms full. "Look what they gave me," he said, "almonds, dates, pistachio nuts. . ."

"I'm not sure I understand," shrugged Saddam. "Weren't they angry?"

"No, they cheered and gave me these presents."

"What exactly did you tell them?"

"All I said was, 'Allah is Great! The jackass is dead!'"

Deep in his palatial bunker, Saddam was selecting his wardrobe for the Mother of All Battles.

"Your Excellency," suggested his valet, "when Napoleon was in Russia he wore a red uniform so that if he was wounded his men would not notice he was bleeding."

"That's an excellent idea!" said Saddam. "Give me my brown pants."

At his command headquarters on the eve of the battle, Saddam huddled with his generals.

"One road leads to defeat, humiliation and total ruin," he told them, "the other to unimaginable destruction. I only hope we have the wisdom to choose correctly."

Military Merriment

Intelligence analysts compiled a psychological profile of Saddam. He harbors deep-seated hatred for his mother, mostly because she has a much better mustache.

During the final hours of Operation Desert Storm, Saddam sent this urgent communique to his troops on the front lines in Kuwait:

"Oh, mighty warriors! I must have volunteers! Just a few brave Iraqi men who will retreat a little slower!"

Private Baxter approached a Bedouin riding a camel along the military road, his aged wife trudging ahead of him.

"Hey, Hassan," said the soldier, "I've been noticing for months that you always ride and your wife always walks. Why is that?"

"Because," replied the Arab, "she has no camel."

"But why does she always walk out in front of you? An old Arab custom?"

"No. Land mines."

WAR

An armed conflict which makes
soldiers change nearly all their
ideas, except their opinion of officers.

After troops piled into Saudi Arabia, a company colonel received an urgent request to receive Private Whitman. Permission was granted.

"Sir," said Whitman, "I gotta have me a three-day pass."

"Well," replied the officer, "you're hardly entitled to it, but I'll listen to your story and it better be good."

"Well, you see sir, my wife's in the army, too. She just got here and she was promoted to top sergeant. And now I got that rare opportunity to do what other soldiers in this man's army have dreamed of doing for the last 100 years."

Mrs. Rosenberg, a wealthy Israeli widow, invited twenty-five soldiers from the encampment near Tel Aviv home for a party. Shortly after they arrived she served cookies and lemonade. A little later in the evening she served cookies and lemonade again. It wasn't long after the second serving that Mrs. Rosenberg announced, "Boys, I have some more cookies left. Now what shall I do with them?"

Sergeant Stobart jumped up and said, "The first guy that answers gets court martialed."

A combined base of British and American army units was stationed together for Operation Desert Storm. After a few months the head of the American sector told his British colleague: "Your boys seem to be having a calming effect on us Americans. The G.I.'s seem to be quieting down a little."

Just then a soldier came running up. Tapping the American general on the shoulder, he asked, "Hey, general, can I borrow your Humvee?"

"See what I mean?" the American told the shocked Briton. "Six months ago he wouldn't have asked."

A troupe of show girls was entertaining the troops at a remote desert camp. They had been at it all afternoon and were not only tired but extremely hungry. Finally, at the close of their performance, the major approached them and asked, "Would you girls like to mess with the enlisted men or the officers this evening?"

"It really doesn't make any difference," spoke up a shapely blonde, "but golly gee, we've just got to have something to eat first."

Sergeant Whittaker barged into the recruits' barracks at Fort Rucker. "All right, you bastards, fall in on the double!" he barked.

Each G.I. grabbed his hat and jumped to his feet except one — a young private who lay in his bunk reading a book. "Well?" roared the sergeant.

"Well," replied the G.I., "there certainly were a lot of them, weren't there?"

Military Merriment

A marine on leave walked into a recruiting station, sought out the recruiting sergeant, and whispered, "Listen, would you mind giving me that big sales talk again. I'm getting a little discouraged."

Wiggins, a recent recruit, was loafing behind the barracks when Sergeant Blythe appeared.

"What are you doing here?" barked the three-striper.

"I'm procrastinating," answered the recruit.

"Okay," said Blythe, "just as long as you keep busy."

OFFICER: Are you happy now that you're in the army?

SOLDIER: Yes, sir.

OFFICER: What were you before you got into the army?

SOLDIER: Much happier.

Colonel Cross was chatting with a young second lieutenant in the Fort McClellan officers' club when a major approached. He coughed politely and said, "I'd like to speak to the colonel about a matter of some importance."

"Go ahead," said Cross.

"If you don't mind, sir, I'd rather not in front of the lieutenant," said the major.

"Well," observed the colonel, "spell it, then."

Tiggets was a poor kid brought up in inner city slums, and could never quite get over it. One day, after he enlisted in the army, Sergeant Gunther caught him eating out of the garbage cans.

"Listen, you," roared the angry sarge, "you'll eat in the mess hall. You're no better than the rest of us."

Kendricks and Peacock, two gyrenes on KP duty, were laboriously trundling a steaming soup kettle from the kitchen. An arrogant marine major stopped them.

"Give me a ladle," he ordered. He tasted. Then he screamed, "You call that soup?"

"No sir, we call that dishwater."

SENTRY: Who goes there?
VOICE: You wouldn't recognize me. I'm new here.

Porterfield was the roughest, toughest, most demanding and hated colonel in the army. Especially during inspection.

One day he marched up and down the ranks, his eyes searching for a slip somewhere. Porterfield stopped in front of a young private, stared at him long and hard, put his face up to the kid's nose and yelled, "Soldier, straighten that tie!"

"You want me to straighten the tie right now, Colonel?" asked the soldier.

"Yes," boomed the colonel, "right now!"

The young G.I. broke his stance, quietly laid his rifle on the ground, reached over, and straightened the colonel's tie.

The armed forces radio announcer finished his daily newscast and was ready to sign off. As usual he closed with the correct time. "For you navy men," he said, "it's now eight bells. For you men in the army, it's oh eight hundred. And for all you officers," he added, "the little hand is on the eight and the big hand is on the twelve."

Colonel McCrae called Private Werner into his office.

"Yesterday, when I passed you on the company street," said the officer, "why didn't you salute me?"

"Well, sir," said Werner, "I guess I just didn't see you."

"Thank heavens! Thank goodness!" said McCrae, "I was afraid you were mad at me!"

Military Merriment

During a battle, the general noticed that one of his soldiers seemed to be devoted to him and followed him everywhere. Finally he remarked, "Soldier, you have stuck by me well during this engagement."

"Yes, sir," said the G.I. "My old mama back in Alabama told me to be sure and stick with the generals and I'd never get hurt."

In basic training at Fort Benning, Lieutenant Stoller was fed up with Brink, a recruit. "Without a doubt, you're the stupidest guy in the service," roared the officer.

"Sorry, I can't help it, sir," replied the recruit. "I was born that way."

"Just answer me two simple questions," continued the lieutenant. "First — what would happen if one of your ears was shot off?"

"That's easy, sir," replied the G.I. "I wouldn't be able to hear."

"Okay," said Stoller. "Next — what would happen if both your ears were shot off?"

"Then I couldn't see," answered Brink.

"What do you mean?" yelled the officer.

"Well, sir," explained the G.I., "if my ears was both shot off, my helmet would slide down over my eyes."

Markland and Crump, two old soldiers, met in a Portland park. "Say," asked Markland, "whatever happened to Sergeant Dye, the guy who used to soak his feet in a pail of water every time he got a chance?"

"Oh," answered Crump, "seems he's down in Faye, Arkansas. He's got a little place there and he just spends his time wading around in a little creek on his property."

"I suppose he ain't even thinkin' about soldierin' or the army now, huh?"

"Oh, no," said Crump. "Old Dye never soldiers. He just wades at Faye."

"Hello. This is the Eighth Army Corps Depot."

"Hello. We need twelve vehicles in the parade square immediately, two of them must be limousines."

"What are the limousines for? To haul those fat-slob generals around in, I bet."

"Soldier, do you know who this is speaking?"

"No, I don't."

"This is General Gelder at this end."

"Do you know who this is speaking, sir?"

"No, I don't."

"See ya 'round ... fatso."

Zack was assigned as chauffeur to Colonel Crockett, a bachelor who had a keen eye for the ladies. While driving down main street one afternoon, Crockett spotted a gorgeous blonde strolling in the opposite direction. "Turn the car around, on the double," ordered the officer, "and pull up alongside that young lady."

Zack clumsily stalled the engine, then had so much trouble getting it started again the blonde had disappeared in the crowd.

"Good grief, soldier," snapped Crockett, "you'd be a total loss in an emergency."

"No, I wouldn't sir," said Zack. "That was my girl."

MESS SERGEANT:	Let me tell you something, wise guy! I was baking pies before you were born.
PRIVATE FOSS:	Well, okay, but why serve them now?

"I suppose," snarled the leathery sergeant to Private Gill, "that when you're discharged from the army, you'll wait for me to die, just so you can spit on my grave."

"Not me," observed Gill. "When I get out of the army, I never want to stand in line again."

Military Merriment

During his first furlough, a newly commissioned army second lieutenant discovered that he had no change with which to buy cigarettes at a vending machine. Catching sight of a passing marine, he motioned him over. "Do you have change for a dollar?" he asked.

"I'm pretty sure I do," said the Marine, searching through his pockets.

"Just a minute," snapped the lieutenant. "That's no way to reply to an officer. Now, let's try it again. Do you have change for a dollar, private?"

The young marine came to attention, saluted smartly and said, "No, sir."

POTENTIAL NCO:
(at examination)   Sir, I have neither pencil nor paper.
INSTRUCTOR: What would you think of a soldier who went to battle without a rifle or ammunition?
POTENTIAL NCO: Well, I would think he was an officer, sir.

A class of G.I.s about to become sergeants was listening to a particularly boring lecture by Sergeant McCluskey, who was currently making life miserable for them.

"A good sergeant," he bellowed, "can't be made ... a good sergeant has to be born. Any questions?"

"Yeah, sarge. Is that in or out of wedlock?"

Captain Criswell of the 5th Regiment was being questioned about the heroic exploits of one of his men. "What made you pick Boles for the mission, sir?"

The officer replied, "When I saw him eating strawberry shortcake while watching an army film on hygiene, I knew he had guts."

The 82nd Airborne troops were being taught how to use their parachutes.

"What if it doesn't open?" asked one rookie.

"That, soldier, is known as jumping to a conclusion!"

PARACHUTE JUMPER'S SONG

It don't mean a thing — if you don't pull the string.

Corrigan had never jumped from an airplane before and was getting his last-minute instructions from the sergeant.

"Count ten and pull the first cord. If by some chance that doesn't work, pull the second cord for your extra parachute. Now, when you land, remember there'll be a truck there to pick you up."

Corrigan jumped, counted to ten, and pulled the first rip cord. Nothing happened. He pulled the second — still no parachute. As he fell to the ground the paratrooper muttered, "And now I suppose that damn truck won't be there either."

SUPPLY OFFICER: Does the new uniform fit you?
RECRUIT: The jacket isn't bad, sir, but the trousers are a little loose around the armpits.

Pvt. Boyer, at paratroop training school, asked the first sergeant. "I don't understand something in the manual. It says, 'As you leave the aircraft, be sure you're not jumping on another parachutist—.'"

"That should be obvious to you," said the non-com. "It only takes a minute to look down."

Boyer moaned, "You're kidding! You mean I'm supposed to keep my eyes *open*?"

Military Merriment

Haden, a recruit in Great Lakes, lost his rifle on the firing range. When the chief petty officer said he would have to pay for it, Haden protested.

"Suppose I was driving a Jeep and somebody stole it. Would I have to pay for that too?"

"Yes," snapped the CPO.

"Now," said the recruit, "I know why the captain always goes down with his ship."

A new bunch of enlisted men got seasick over the rail. Soon one of the old salts joined them and sarcastically inquired, "What's the matter, Zander? Got a weak stomach?"

"Hell no," gasped the green-gilled sailor. "I'm throwing it as far as the others."

The oldest first lieutenant in the air force was at least fifty years old. "How come you never got promoted," asked one of his fellow officers.

"It was during Viet Nam," he explained. "Every night the CO insisted on getting us out of bed for an alert. After a couple of months, I found a large monkey in the hills, dressed him in one of my old uniforms, and trained him to run to my plane when the alert sounded, hop in, start the engine, and sit there, ready to go, until the all-clear sounded.

"For weeks it worked great, but one night the all-clear never came, and I rushed out onto the field just in time to see my plane, with the monkey at the controls, taking off from the field and joining the formation. There we were, the CO and I, the only two people left on the field.

"And that's why I'm the oldest first lieutenant in the air force," said the officer, "and frankly, I wouldn't mind it so much — if it weren't for the fact that that damned monkey is now a colonel."

**An old general never lies down
on the job — but his privates usually do.**

135

Seaman Stanton stuttered when he got excited. One night the sailor ran to the captain on the bridge during a storm and started, "P-p-please, s-s-sir. . ."

"Well, what's wrong?" bellowed the captain.

The flustered deckhand tried again but couldn't seem to get past the first two words.

"For Pete's sake, hurry up!" roared the captain. "If you can't say it ... SING IT!"

The deckhand took a deep breath and sang:

"Should old acquaintance be forgot
And never brought to mind,
The admiral's fallen overboard,
He's a half a mile behind!"

OVERHEARD AT A PARTY

"I tried on my old World War II Army
uniform and the only thing that fit were the socks."

The war against the Axis was nearly at an end. Some enlisted men were having a beer at a cafe near Fort Dix. When the topic got off girls, they started to talk about soldiering. Most of them were bitter about being drafted. One said, "Sure, you know who didn't have to get into uniform — the sons of the big shots! Their daddies used their pull!"

From the next table, a voice said, "Guys, you're all wrong. I've been in two months ... all kinds of men get taken into the army. My dad's a senator and I'm here!"

The other soldiers nodded and said, "Well, maybe you're right, Major Tulbert!"

At the edge of a forest, a patrol was taking a beating from enemy small arms fire. A reporter joined them and asked, "Why don't you hide behind the trees?"

One of the soldiers said, "We're enlisted men. They don't even have enough trees for the officers!"

Lieutenant Leyton, the officer of the day, told Private Wattle, the guard at the entrance to Fort Leavenworth, "Look real sharp! Any minute now, a five-star general will be coming through."

Wattle marched up and down for an hour. The lieutenant returned and asked, "Did General Thornton show up yet?"

"No, sir."

He came back an hour later. "Any sign of the general?"

"No, sir."

Finally, at about midnight, in rode General Thornton. The guard raised his hand, stopped the command car and asked, "Who goes there?"

"General Thornton."

Wattle snapped to attention, saluted smartly and said, "You're late, General. And boy, are you going to get it from the lieutenant!"

A famous admiral and an equally famous general were fishing together during World War II when a sudden squall came up. When it died down both eminent warriors were struggling helplessly in the water.

The admiral floundered his way back to the boat and finally pulled himself in. Then, using an oar, he fished out the general.

"Please don't say a word about this to anyone," puffed the admiral. "If the navy found out that I couldn't swim I'd be disgraced."

"Don't worry," said the general. "Your secret is safe. I'd hate to have my men find out I can't walk on water."

Woody and Nick, two World War II vets, were having a brew at the American Legion Hall.

"You remember the pills they gave us in the trenches to keep our minds off women?" asked Woody.

"I do," said Nick, "and what's more, I think they're beginning to work."

An admiral was in a Quantico, Virginia naval hospital with nothing worse than athlete's foot and non-critical complications. He spent his time chasing nurses, pulling rank on enlisted patients, and harassing the overworked medical staff.

This went on until Metzler, a young marine, borrowed a surgical gown, cap and face mask, and swept into the admiral's room. "Good morning," said Metzler. He glanced quickly at the chart, then ordered the patient up on his hands and knees and proceeded to take his temperature.

Before Metzler could finish the job, the marine explained, "There's another urgent case I've got to get to. Don't move until I return."

One hour later the head nurse, making her rounds, froze at the naval officer's doorway.

"Admiral!" she gasped. "What — what happened?"

"Taking my temperature," growled the navy man. "Anything unusual about taking an admiral's temperature?"

"N-no, sir," stammered the nurse, "but, Admiral — with a daffodil?"

SAILOR

A man who makes his living
on water but never touches it on land.

Orville and his wife were watching TV together in the living room one evening. The phone rang, Orville picked it up and said, "How on earth should I know? Why don't you call the Coast Guard?"

The wife asked, "Who was that, dear?"

Orville said, "I have no idea. Some stupid jerk wanted to know if the coast was clear."

A giant blue whale fell in love with a submarine and constantly followed it around the ocean. One day the submarine fired a torpedo, and the whale passed out cigars.

Military Merriment

"All right, does anyone aboard this submarine know how to pray?"

"I do."

"Good. You pray. The rest of us will put on escape lungs. We're short one."

A navy recruiter failed dismally in persuading a likely young prospect to sign up for submarine duty.

"Thank you kindly," said the Texan, "but I ain't shipping out on any vessel that sinks on purpose."

A famous admiral had been the hero of numerous encounters battling Germans in the Mediterranean and convoy landings in the South Pacific. But his officers noticed that the great admiral had a strange idiosyncrasy. Each morning after breakfast he would go to his stateroom, open his safe and read a message. Finally one day, several officers got up the courage and dared to go into his cabin. They opened the safe and looked at the little note he read every day. It said: "Starboard is right, Port is left."

The first mate was leaning over the ship's rail trying to comfort a suffering sailor. "Cheer up, kid," he said. "Nobody ever died of seasickness."

"Don't say that," groaned the sailor. "It's only the hope of dying that's kept me alive so far!"

The commanding officer at the San Diego recruit center had a very hard time with the enlistees and he said angrily, "No man in this outfit will be given liberty today."

Somewhere in the crowd a voice rang out, "Give me liberty or give me death!"

The CO turned red and barked, "Who said that?"

"Patrick Henry," said another voice.

Harker and Frye, on leave in Honolulu, were watching a hula girl wriggle.

"Did you know," remarked Harker, "that those hip motions tell a whole story?"

"You don't say!" exclaimed Frye. "And to think of all the time I wasted reading books!"

At Fort Bliss, Colonel Kessler, Major Morton and Captain Carruthers were having an argument. The heated discussion centered around the percentage of pleasure and work involved in making love.

"I believe," said the colonel, "that lovemaking is 50 percent pleasure and 50 percent work."

"I hate to disagree with you, sir," said the major, "but I think it's 60 percent pleasure and 40 percent work."

"Gentlemen," said the captain, "you are entitled to your opinions, but I believe that making love is 80 percent pleasure and 20 percent work."

"Let's settle it right now," said the colonel. "Here comes a new recruit. Young man!"

"Yes, sir!" answered the saluting soldier.

"We'd like you to help us settle an argument we're having. What percentage of lovemaking is pleasure and how much is work?"

"Colonel, I believe it's 100 percent pleasure. 'Cause if there was any work involved you guys would have had me doing it a long time ago."

WEDDED WHIMSY

**If it weren't for marriage, husbands
and wives would have to fight with strangers.**

"What makes you so sure your wife doesn't like you
any more?"
"She went out and bought me a deerskin coat to wear
when I go hunting."

A motorcycle cop pulled along side an auto and shouted,
"Pull over to the curb. You don't have a taillight."
The motorist stepped out, looked in back of the car and
began shaking and quivering uncontrollably. "Take it easy,"
said the policeman, "it's not that bad."
"It's not the taillight I'm worrying about," cried the
motorist. "Where's my wife and the trailer?"

Chuck and Spence were sitting beside each other at a bar having a brew. "How'd you meet your wife?" asked Chuck.

"I met her at a dance," replied Spence.

"That must have been romantic."

"No, embarrassing," said Spence. "She told me she was taking the kids and going home to her mother."

MARRIED MAN

A fellow who wishes he were as
smart as he thinks his wife thinks he is.

"Who introduced you to your husband?"

"We just happened to meet. I don't blame anybody."

MRS. COLE: Bob took me dancing last night.

MRS. BART: I never thought of your husband as
a dancer. Is he light on his feet?

MRS. COLE: His, yes ... mine, no.

Mrs. Bartlett was bent over the breakfast table in pain. "My head aches," she moaned, "I've a terrible pain in my stomach and my left breast burns as if it's on fire."

"It's all right honey," soothed the hubby. "Here's an aspirin for your head, Alka-Seltzer for your stomach and if you'll lift your breast out of the hot coffee, I'm sure it won't hurt so much."

**There's only one way to make
a happy marriage, and most husbands
and wives would like to know what it is.**

Wedded Whimsey

The Wimples were ready to go to sleep. After the wife got into bed, Wimple approached his wife holding a glass of water in one hand and some aspirin in the other.

"What's this?" she asked.

"Aspirin," he answered.

"Aspirin? But I don't have a headache," she replied.

"Gotcha!" said Wimple.

Metcalfe phoned his wife from the office one afternoon and said, "I've got two tickets for the theater."

"That's just wonderful, darling," she exclaimed. "I'll hurry and start dressing at once."

"Yes, please do," he said patiently. "The tickets are for tomorrow night."

Hutchinson had a roving eye. At a party he kept watching every move of a young blonde in a very revealing gown, with a neckline cut down almost to the waist.

His wife took it as long as she could. Finally she leaned over to her husband's ear and said, "I'll bet if you saw her kitchen sink, you'd find that's well stacked too!"

WARD: Are you married?

MILO: No, I look this way because somebody just stole my car.

Macklin and Flack were eating their lunch on the construction site. "You have a good time with your wife this summer?" Macklin asked.

"Naw," said Flack. "She went all the places I did."

A good husband is the light of his wife's life, and a smart wife doesn't let her light go out every night.

Shelby and Jennifer were battling it out over breakfast.

"I never thought it was possible for one woman to be so beautiful and yet so stupid," said Shelby.

"It's God's will," said his wife. "He made me beautiful so I'd be attractive to you. He made me stupid so you'd be attractive to me."

MARRIAGE

The only state that allows
a woman to work 18 hours a day.

"It's just too damn hot to wear clothes today," said Shane, stepping out of the shower. "Honey, what do you think all of our neighbors would say if I mowed the lawn like this?"

"Probably that I married you for your money."

HUSBAND: Wouldn't it be fun to go to the Holy Land and stand on Mount Sinai and shout out the Ten Commandments?

WIFE: It would be better if you stayed home and kept them.

What are the two stages of being a husband?

When you want to be faithful but are not, and when you want to be unfaithful and cannot.

Russell dashed into his wife's bedroom, livid with anger. "You miserable woman!" he screamed. "I know everything now!"

"All right, big shot!" she said. "When was the Battle of Bunker Hill?"

Wedded Whimsey

Bushnell lived in Connecticut and commuted each day to his Manhattan office. After forty years of catching the same early morning train he finally retired. The next morning he told his wife not to turn his fried eggs over because he didn't like them that way.

"My dear," she exclaimed, "why on earth didn't you ever tell me that before?"

"Frankly," he replied, "I never had the time."

Roseanne was trying to persuade her husband to rent a cottage in Virginia Beach during his summer vacation instead of going on their usual trip to Chicago.

"But honey, you'll just be stuck in the kitchen, cooking and cleaning."

"That's okay, sweetheart," she said. "All I want is a change of sinks."

Astrid and Lucas were having another of their spats. "You think you know it all, don't you?" snarled the husband. "Well, I'll tell you this ... I'm nobody's fool."

"Really?" she said. "Then maybe you should get someone to adopt you!"

Why is marriage like a warm toilet seat?

It's comfortable, but you never know who was there before you.

Hank swiftly climbed the ladder and tapped on the window pane of his beloved's bedroom.

"Are yawl packed?" he called.

"Hush," said the girl. "Daddy may hear yew. Ah think he's just in the next room."

"Can't be," said the young man. "He's holdin' the ladder."

145

Gus and Rusti were discussing reincarnation. "I don't know if I'd rather come back wealthy or handsome," said the husband.

"Well darling," replied Rusti, "either way would be a great improvement."

WIFE:
(at the bedside of sick husband)   Is there no hope, doctor?

DOCTOR: I don't know. What are you hoping for?

Fern and Grace were discussing ways of controlling the nocturnal wanderings of their spouses. "I've got the perfect cure for my husband," said Fern. "When I hear him fumbling around downstairs, I call out, 'Is that you Carl?'"

"So how does that cure him?" asked Grace.

"His name is Brad."

Maxine was about to die so she made a last request of her husband, Les. "At the funeral," she begged, "please let my mother ride with you in the first car."

"All right," said Les, "but it'll ruin the day for me."

Mildred was complaining to her spouse about the ill manners of a friend who had just left. "If that woman yawned once while I was talking, she yawned ten times."

"Maybe she wasn't yawning, dear," replied the husband. "Perhaps she was trying to say something."

**Never try to keep up with
the Joneses; they might be newlyweds.**

Wedded Whimsey

Sheik Kamal Al-Assad was the guest at a chic party when he admitted to his female dinner partner that he indeed did have four wives as the Koran permits.

"That's the ultimate in male chauvinism," the woman lashed out. "Imagine having more than one wife just in case you get tired of the same woman! Did it ever occur to you that a woman just might grow tired of you too?"

"That," said the Arab, "is what the other three are for."

"I think I can explain why my husband feels down in the mouth," said a housewife. "Somehow, I forgot to take the feathers off the duck we had for dinner."

Cal's nagging wife was finding fault with him as usual.

"This is the last straw," she threatened finally. "I swear, I'm going to divorce you."

"Now dear," said Cal, "I know you don't mean it. You're just saying that to make me feel good."

HUEY: How did you get that black eye?
JAKE: Our new maid is ticklish.
HUEY: Did she sock you?
JAKE: No. My wife did when she heard
           the maid giggle.

Phillip was past fifty and had spent the best years of his life with a woman whose constant criticism had driven him mad. Now, in poor health, his business on the verge of bankruptcy, he made up his mind. He went to the dining room, fastened his tie over the chandelier, and was about to end it all. At that moment his wife entered the room.

She stood shocked at the scene before her, then cried, "Phillip, that's your best tie!"

147

Doctor Garwood had finished administering to a sick little boy and assured his mother that he'd recover soon. As they walked through the living room the M.D. commented on the beauty of the home. "That's a particularly beautiful vase. Tell me about it."

"It contains my husband's ashes," said the woman.

"Oh, I'm sorry. How long has he been dead?"

"He's not. Just too lazy to find an ashtray."

"Does your husband help you with the baby?"

"Sure. Right now he's taking a nap for him."

Ruthanne and Suzy were talking about their husbands. "I'm more and more convinced that my husband married me for my money," said Ruthanne.

"Then you have the satisfaction of knowing that he's not as stupid as he looks," replied Suzy.

WIFE: I'm going to enter a contest. They're giving prizes for completing a sentence in 15 words or less.

HUSBAND: I'll give you a prize myself if you can finish any sentence in 15 words or less.

"Mickey seems to have a good marriage."

"Yeah, he admits his wife controls the kids, the cat and the canary, but he can say whatever he likes to the goldfish."

George and Myra, leaving for Florida, were being bid farewell by some friends. One fellow said to George, "It gets pretty hot in Florida. Aren't you afraid the climate might disagree with Myra?"

"It wouldn't dare," signed the husband.

148

Wedded Whimsey

Newbold was a typical nagging husband. One day his wife couldn't take it anymore and finally erupted.

"All right, so I like to spend money," cried Mrs. Newbold, "but name one other extravagance!"

MATRIMONY

An institution in which half the husbands
do not half appreciate their better halves.

Stay-at-home wife: "Darling, how very thoughtful of the hotel where you stayed in San Diego during the convention. They sent me a beautiful blue nightgown."

Harriet stormed angrily into the neighborhood post office and informed the postmaster, "Mister, your department is inexcusably inefficient. My husband went to Portland on business last week and I just got a letter from him postmarked Las Vegas!"

Cheryl went shopping for a gift for her husband. After looking at cuff links, golf clubs, sportswear and video games she realized he had all those things. She finally decided to get him an ash tray.

The department store clerk showed her several dozen but nothing pleased her. Finally she pointed to a large ash can and asked the price.

"Excuse me, but that's no ash tray," said the clerk. "That's an ash can."

"Oh, that's quite all right," she replied. "My husband is very nearsighted."

Binky and Danielle were to be married soon and were planning their honeymoon.

"Honey, what about a cruise to Bermuda?" he asked.

"I'd love it," she replied, "except you know how terribly seasick I get."

"Making love is the best cure for seasickness."

"Yes, darling," said the bride-to-be, "but think of the return trip."

HUSBAND: My wife does bird imitations.
FRIEND: For instance?
HUSBAND: She watches me like a hawk.

Geraldine felt neglected and she finally got up the courage to complain to her husband. "Just because we've been married for 20 years doesn't mean you can take me for granted," she sniffed. "Why I'll have you know that when I was young I could have married a real caveman."

"Of course," said her husband. "When you were young that's all there were!"

"Luke, are you married?"

"No. I was married once. Now I just lease."

Jeff was complaining to his friend Phil.

"When I was first married, I was the happiest man in the world. When I came home at night my wife would fetch my slippers while my little dog would run around the room barking at me. After five years everything's changed. Now the dog brings me my slippers and my wife runs around the room barking at me!"

"What are you complaining about?" shrugged his friend. "You're still getting the same service."

Wedded Whimsey

Judi confessed to Melinda during their lunch break. "I'm fed up with living with Trent. That creep hasn't so much as kissed me since the honeymoon!"

"For heaven's sake!" said Melinda emphatically. "Then why don't you divorce the guy?"

"How can I?" moaned Judi. "We're not married."

The television game show emcee was talking to a contestant who was a photographer.

CONTESTANT: I've been taking wedding pictures for years.

TV EMCEE: Tell me, at a wedding, who would you say smiles the most, the bride or the groom?

CONTESTANT: The bride's father.

Reverend Pettigrew asked for anyone in the congregation who knew a truly perfect person to stand up. After a long pause, a meek-looking fellow in the back arose.

"Do you really know a perfect person?" queried the shocked minister.

"Yes, sir, I do," answered the little man.

"Won't you please tell the congregation who the rare perfect person is?" asked Pettigrew.

"Yes, sir. My wife's first husband."

Roslyn was happily showing off her new mink coat. "My goodness, that sure was nice of your husband to buy you that fur coat," said her friend, Glenda.

"He had to," replied Roslyn. "The other night I caught him kissing the maid."

"How dreadful. Did you fire her?"

"No," she smiled. "I still need a new purse and shoes."

**Divorce has done more
to promote peace than the U.N.**

Carla came to Ty in tears. "The woman next door has a pair of shoes exactly like mine."

"I suppose," grumbled her husband, "you think you have to buy another pair?"

"Well," said Carla, "it would be a little cheaper than moving, wouldn't it?"

Mrs. Whitney was jubilant. "I've finally cured my husband of biting his nails," she declared.

"That's swell," said her neighbor. "How?"

"I hide his teeth."

MARRIAGE LICENSE

What some liberated
women never had, and
would like their daughters to have.

Pregnant Mrs. Potter told her spouse he had better get her to the hospital. The harried husband immediately rushed to the phone and called the Seton Medical Center. Potter said he was bringing his wife in and that they should notify the doctor that she was ready to deliver.

"Is this her first baby?" asked the nurse.

"Of course not," he screamed. "This is her husband!"

Foster decided to surprise his wife with a trip to Puerta Vallarta for a second honeymoon.

On the first night they were standing out on the balcony of their hotel room and she said, "Gee, honey this is great. There's a full moon, I've got on a sexy nightgown, we've been drinking champagne, all the kids are back home — I just wish the piano was here."

"What do we need the piano for?"

She said, "That's where I left my birth control pills."

Wedded Whimsey

Mrs. Scotti, a Detroit mother of eight children, was telling Hunt, the foreman at the plant, "There's never any trouble at our house. My husband works the night shift and I work days, so there's always one of us at home with the kids all the time."

"That's fine for the youngsters," said Hunt, "but it doesn't leave you much time for each other."

"It certainly doesn't," she agreed. "As he's coming in the front door, I'm going out the back."

"Then how'd you come to have eight children?" asked the foreman.

"Sometimes I don't make it through the door in time."

NEWS ITEM

Mrs. Kathleen O'Doul, a Dublin housewife, last night gave birth to her twelfth child. Mrs. O'Doul was quoted in the delivery room as saying that she has "had her feet in the stirrups more times than John Wayne."

What did the lady say when her husband announced that he was going to become a necrophiliac?

"Over my dead body!"

Mrs. Welland invited her new neighbors, the Garnetts, in for tea. She poured a cup for the husband and asked if he took sugar.

"No," he said.

"Yes," said Mrs. Garnett at the same moment. Then she turned to him. "But I always put sugar in your tea."

"I know," said Garnett. "I used to remind you not to. Now I just don't stir."

153

Maurine was eyeing the expensive fur coat of a Hollywood producer's wife.

"I can't help," she sneered, "pitying the poor beast who suffered in order that you might get it."

"How dare you speak that way of my husband!" snapped the woman angrily.

FROM THE EDITORIAL PAGE OF A NEBRASKA NEWSPAPER

Dear Editor:
I have read recently that the word "obey" is now being omitted from the wedding ceremony. May I ask if you think the new wording for the wedding service is retroactive?

Did you hear about the man who owned a lot of sheep and wanted to take them over a river that was all ice, but the woman who owned the river said, "No!"

So he promised to marry her and that's how he pulled the wool over her ice.

NEW HUSBAND: Did you sew the button on my shirt, darling?

NEW WIFE: No, dear, I couldn't find the button, so I just sewed up the buttonhole.

From upstairs Mrs. Danton called down to the unlit living room where Greg was sitting with his girlfriend. "What are you doing down there, son?" she demanded.

"Nothing, Mom," he called back.

"You're getting more like your father every day!"

Wedded Whimsey

"Doctor, my husband talks in his sleep," complained Arlene to her family physician.

"That's easy enough to fix," he replied. "Just give him one of these pills every night before he retires, he'll be cured in no time."

"I don't want to cure him," she exclaimed. "He's very interesting. I want something to keep *me* awake."

Marilyn bought a lottery ticket every week for a year and a miracle finally happened. She hit the jackpot. She called her husband immediately and said, "Honey, I won ten million dollars. Start packing."

Her husband said, "That's terrific. Should I pack summer clothes for a cruise or winter clothes for skiing?"

She said, "Pack everything! I want you out of the house by tomorrow morning!"

MARITAL MELODY

Hurray! I have found the solution!
Yes, I've finally delved to the source;
And now it can be told that marriage
Is the principal cause of divorce.

Nolan fell asleep to the steady drone of his wife's voice. Suddenly she was shaking him violently.

"Come on, wake up," she shrieked. "You're talking in your sleep."

Nolan shook his sleepy head. "For heaven's sake," he yawned, "you can't possibly begrudge me those few words, can you?"

Divorce is useless. You marry for lack of judgement, you divorce for lack of patience, then you remarry for lack of money.

A famous movie star, several times divorced, was granted her latest decree. On the steps of the courthouse a reporter stopped her.

"How do you feel?" asked the reporter.

"I feel like a new man," she replied.

Mountford, a successful Wall Street broker, liked to putter around his Connecticut garden. Wearing his oldest clothes, he was cheerfully trimming the hedges one Sunday afternoon when an older woman stopped her Mercedes at the curb and hailed him.

"What do you get for being the gardener here?" she asked. "Perhaps I can offer you more to come with me."

"I don't think so," said Mountford. "The lady who lives here lets me sleep with her."

At breakfast one morning Polly asked Sterling, "Do you know what day this is?"

Her husband had no idea, but felt he should know. "Course I do!" he answered.

Sterling thought about it all the way to work. Her birthday? No. Anniversary? No. Something to do with the kids? No.

It was on his mind all day.

The anniversary of our first date? When I proposed? What could it be? He could take no chances. That night Sterling came home with flowers, took Polly out to dinner, and later gave her diamond ear clips.

"Did I remember today?" he asked with a smile.

"You certainly did," she said. "You've made this the happiest Ground Hog's Day I've ever had."

SENIOR SNICKERS

A senior citizen is a person who remembers when a senior citizen was called an old-timer.

Dr. Horvath gave Polin, his eighty-year-old patient, a complete physical examination.

"I've been practicing for two decades," said the M.D., "and I'm darned if anybody has ever come to me before with a complaint like yours. What do you mean, 'your virility's too high?'"

"It's all up in my head," sighed the senior.

At eighty, there are six women for every man. What a time to get odds like that!

Debbs had been driving down the Northern California coast in a dense fog. He was following a taillight and crashed into the car ahead of him when it stopped suddenly.

"Why didn't you let me know you were going to stop?" yelled Debbs angrily.

"Why should I?" came a voice booming out of the fog. "I'm in my own garage!"

Just for fun, old Hargrove decided to have his fortune told. He sat before the elderly Gypsy woman eagerly awaiting her predictions.

The crystal-gazer clasped her hands and informed him excitedly, "I see a buried treasure."

"I know," nodded Hargrove. "My wife's first husband."

One sunny Florida morning in St. Petersburg, Mrs. Sanster shook her retired husband awake. "How about helping me straighten up the house?" she asked.

"Why?" replied her husband. "Is it tilted?"

Up the road in Clearwater, Kriegel, another retiree, was shuffling along, bent over at the waist, as his wife helped him into the doctor's waiting room. A woman in the office viewed the scene with sympathy.

"Arthritis with complications?" she asked.

The wife shook her head. "Do-it-yourself," she explained, "with concrete blocks."

Monte and Brien were playing checkers in a Winter Park seniors recreation center. "How old do you think that widow Mrs. Cronin is?" asked Monte.

"Her age is her own business," answered Brien, "but it looks like she's been in the business a long time."

Lerman, aged 75, rushed into a doctor's office. "You gotta give me a shot so I should be young again," he pleaded. "I got a date with a young chicken tonight!"

"Just a minute," said the physician, "you're 75 years old. There's nothing I can do for you!"

"But doctor," exclaimed the old man, "my good friend, Rosen, is over 85, and he says that he makes love three times a week!"

"All right," advised the doctor, "so you *say* it too."

OPTIMIST

An 89-year-old bachelor who gets married and
starts looking for a house close to a school.

Did you hear about the Phoenix retiree who goes horseback riding every day of the year except for the month of June?

That's when the man who puts him up on the horse goes on vacation!

Whittle, an eager-beaver young real estate agent, was doing his best to sell old Cantrowitz a condominium in Miami Beach. Having outlined its many attractions, Whittle concluded his pitch, "Remember, Mister Cantrowitz, this is an investment in the future."

"Sonny," croaked the old man, "at my age I don't even buy green bananas."

**For most seniors, old
age is fifteen years from now!**

Mrs. Brack had been a widow for some time. One day she walked into a photo shop and said to the owner, "I'd like to have this picture of my poor dead husband fixed up."

"What is it you want done?" asked the proprietor.

"Well, this picture is the only one that I have of him, but he's wearing a hat," explained the widow. "I want you to take the hat off so I can see his gorgeous hair."

"What kind of hair did he have?"

"Take off that hat and you'll see!" replied Mrs. Brack.

During the tensest moment of a murder movie, white-haired Holman began groping around for something on the theatre floor. He completely disturbed a lady in the next seat.

"What have you lost?" she inquired sharply.

"A caramel," said Holman.

"You're going to all this bother for a caramel?"

"Yes," said the retiree, "my teeth are in it."

Sally, the waitress in a Savannah restaurant, stood near a table watching an unusual occurrence. She wondered why an elderly man plowed through a heavy dinner while his wife sat drumming her fingers on the tablecloth and gazing out of the window.

Finally, Sally asked the woman, "Aren't you hungry?"

"You bet I am," said the wife, "but I gotta wait till Pa's finished with the teeth."

She had been putting it off for years. Each of her six children pleaded and then together they all insisted. Finally, old Mrs. Kazinski had some dentures made. Three days later she returned to Dr. Wallach's office.

"You know those teeth you made for me?" she asked. "They're no good. They don't fit."

"That's not too unusual," replied the dentist. "Let's check your bite and see what the trouble is."

After performing several bite tests, Wallach announced, "As far as I can see they fit fine!"

"I'm not talking about my mouth," said the woman, "they don't fit in the glass."

Strickfaden, age 83, sat in the doctor's waiting room and was soon ushered into the physician's office. "All right," said the M.D., "what seems to be the trouble?"

"You're the one who went to school for ten years," snapped the senior. "You tell me!"

Did you hear about the fearless septuagenarian hunter in the jungles of Ceylon who was so anxious to bag a leopard that, in the excitement, his false teeth fell out?

Ever since the poor man has been searching for his bridge on the River Kwai.

Then there's the Wichita man whose family claims he's going through a second childhood.

He went to a dentist and had braces put on his dentures.

SIGN IN DENVER DENTIST'S OFFICE

Be true to thy teeth,
and they will not be false to thee.

One evening, Warberg was seated at the same table in Wolfe's Delicatessen on Miami Beach with Rifkin, a retiree. Warberg noticed that the poor man was chewing with nothing but gums so he pulled some false teeth out of his pocket and offered them to Rifkin. They were too loose.

Warberg volunteered another set of dentures. This time they were too tight. The third set, however, fit perfectly.

"Thanks very much!" said Rifkin. "What a pleasure to sit at the same table with such a fine dentist!"

"Whatta ya mean, dentist!" said Warberg indignantly. "I'm an undertaker!"

161

A wealthy Boca Raton socialite was talking to Mendelbaum to see if she could hire him to cut her grass. They had difficulty negotiating a fee, so finally she said, "I'll tell you what. Let's give it a trial — you come to work for me Thursday, and I'll pay you what you're worth."

"That don't make no sense!" send Mendelbaum. "I get more than that from Social Security."

Mrs. Morelli, age 86, walked into a doctor's office.

"What's your complaint?" asked the physician.

"I feel tired and run down!" she said.

"Well, I'm terribly sorry," said the M.D., "but I can't make you younger!"

"All I wanna you to do," said Mrs. Morelli, "is make-a me older!"

"Lieberman must be well on in years!"

"Oh yes, the poor man. He's so old he gets winded playing checkers."

Slodnick passed away at age 82 and within days his relatives gathered like vultures to hear the reading of the will. The lawyer tore open the envelope, drew out a piece of paper and read "Being of sound mind, I made sure I spent every single dime before I died."

The lawyer stood before the family of the recently deceased Morris Schneider and read aloud his will:

"To my dear wife, I leave my house, 50 acres of land and one million dollars.

"To my son Ruby, I leave my two cars and $200,000.

"To my daughter, Sarah, I leave my yacht and $200,000.

"And to my brother-in-law, who always insisted that health is better than wealth, I leave my sun lamp."

Mrs. Krebs was proudly wheeling her granddaughter down Collins Avenue. A friend passed them on the sidewalk and stopped her, peeked into the carriage and cried, "Oh my! You've got some gorgeous baby there!"

"You think she's gorgeous!" sniffed Mrs. Krebs. "Wait'll you see her pictures!"

VERNE: Have I told you about my grandchildren?
CARNEY: No, and I thank you very much!

Doctor Cox approached his 83-year-old patient in the hospital room. "Mr. Adler, you're the best patient we've ever had in this hospital, and because you've been so cooperative I'm going to tell you something we don't usually tell a patient. I'm sorry — but you're going to die. Is there anyone you'd like to see?"

"Yes," answered Adler. "I'd like to see another doctor!"

Stein, aged 68, visited the office of his physician son and asked for something that would increase his sexual potency. The M.D. gave his father a shot and refused to accept a fee. Nevertheless, Stein insisted on giving him twenty dollars.

A week later, Stein was back for another injection and this time handed his son fifty dollars.

"But Pop! Shots are only twenty dollars!"

"Take it," said Stein. "The extra is from Mama!"

The widow Powderly returned to her hotel in San Francisco after a day of sightseeing. "I'm sorry," she said to the elderly hotel clerk, "I'm so forgetful. Will you tell me what room I'm in?"

"You're in the lobby," replied the clerk.

On his 75th birthday, Rossi rushed into a physician's office. "Doctor," he exclaimed, "I got a hot date tonight with a 22-year-old girl ... you gotta give me somethin' that'll pep me up!"

The M.D. smiled sympathetically and supplied the old man with a prescription. Later that night, out of curiosity, the medic phoned his elderly patient. "I just wondered, did the medicine help?"

"It's wonderful!" replied Rossi. "Seven times already!"

"That's really great," agreed the doctor. "And what about the girl?"

"The girl?" said Rossi. "She didn't get here yet!"

An Augusta police officer pulled 86-year-old Mrs. Buford over to the curb and implied that her signals were confusing. "First you put your hand out as if you were going to turn left, then you waved your hand up and down, and then you turned right."

Mrs. Buford explained. "Ah decided not to turn left, and when mah hand was goin' up and down, Ah was erasing the left turn."

What would be the least popular song to request at a Golden Agers' dance?

Taps.

A grey-haired woman climbed three flights of stairs, opened a carved mahogany door and walked into an exotically furnished reception room. A gong sounded and out of a cloud of incense appeared a beautiful Oriental girl.

"Do you," the girl said softly, "wish to meet with his omnipotence, the wise, all-knowing, all-seeing guru, Maharishi Naru?"

"Yeah," said the elderly woman. "Tell Seymour his mother is here from the Bronx!"

164

Mrs. Vogel and Mrs. Dubin, two silver-haired ladies, were sitting next to each other poolside at a posh Miami Beach hotel.

"Tell me, darling, have you been through the menopause?" asked Mrs. Vogel.

"The menopause? I haven't even been through the Fontainbleau yet!"

There was an old woman from Kent
Whose nose was remarkably bent;
    One day, they suppose,
    She followed her nose
And nobody knows where she went.

LITTLE TAD: Grandma, can we go to a movie?
GRANDMA: If it isn't a gangster movie.
TAD: It's not. It's *The Dwarf Rats Meet the Fourlegged Zombie Monsters.*
GRANDMA: All right, dear. Just so it isn't about gangsters.

Roydon, a St. Augustine retiree, went to an optician and announced, "Doc, I would like to get my eyes tested for a pair of glasses."

The doctor placed him in front of a card and asked, "Can you read that plainly?"

"No, I can't," replied Roydon.

The doctor moved the card closer and asked, "How about this? Can you read it now?"

"No, I can't."

The doctor took the card and pushed it right under his nose. "Well, can you read it now?"

"No," said Roydon, "I never learned to read."

**You know you're getting
old when you don't care what your
secretary looks like — as long as she can spell.**

Sharpe brought home a backyard swing set for his children and immediately started to assemble it. All the neighborhood kids were anxiously waiting to play on it.

After several hours of reading the directions, attempting to fit bolt A into slot B, etc., he finally gave up and called Bergson, an old handyman working in a neighboring yard.

Bergson came over, threw the directions away, and in a short while, had the swing set completely assembled.

"It's beyond me," said the young father, "how you got it together without even reading the instructions."

"Tell you the truth," replied the old-timer, "I can't read, and when you can't read, you've got to think."

The handsome network television game show host was interviewing Mr. and Mrs. Abraham Tannenbaum on their sixtieth wedding anniversary.

"How old is your wife?" asked the emcee.

"She's 87," said Tannenbaum, "and God willing, she'll live to be a hundred!"

"And how old are you?" inquired the host.

"I'm 87 too," he said proudly, "and God willing, I'll live to be 101."

"But why," asked the tv host, "would you want to live a year longer than your wife?"

"Truthfully, I'd like to have at least one year of peace!"

Little Rafe was taken by his mother to a seance, and on being asked by the medium if there was anyone he would like to speak to, he said, "My grandpa."

Shortly afterwards the medium went into a suitable trance and soon a spooky voice came floating through the air: "This is grandpa speaking from heaven — what is it you would like to know, my boy?"

"Hello, grandpa," said Rafe. "What are you doing in heaven? You're not even dead yet!"

**She was born in the
year of our Lord only knows!**

Senior Snickers

Landis, a kindly white-haired retiree, was strolling down a Ft. Lauderdale street when he noticed a small boy standing on the front steps of a house trying to reach the doorbell. The boy stood on tiptoe, even jumped up as far as he could, but was unable to reach the bell. Landis walked up the stairs, rang the bell and said, "Well, little fella, what now?"

"I don't know what you're gonna do," said the boy, "but I'm gonna run!"

Mildred and Polly were attending a single seniors dance at the Sarasota Recreation Center.

"How have ya been?" asked Mildred.

"I've lost quite a bit of weight," replied Polly.

"I don't see it."

"Sure you don't. I've lost it."

The widow Dunn was taking her first cruise after her husband passed away.

"Hey, you on deck," a passenger called from his cabin. "Has the moon come up yet?"

Mrs. Dunn, hanging over the ship's rail, answered, "No, but be patient. Everything else has!"

D'Agostino sidled up to a blue-haired beauty at a Pasadena neighborhood party. "S'cuse me," he oozed, "but I have to tell you what charming eyes you have."

"Glad you like them. They were a birthday present."

Little Emory's parents were divorced and he was living with his grandparents, the Stuarts. One evening Mrs. Stuart said to her husband, "Emory's teacher says he ought to have an encyclopedia."

"Encyclopedia, my eye," exclaimed Mr. Stuart. "Let him walk to school like I did."

Little Alice was being taken to Florida by her grandparents for Christmas vacation. Aboard a plane that made several intermediate stops, little Alice asked her grandmother, "What was the name of the city before last that we landed in?"

The woman, deeply engrossed in a paperback, grumbled, "How do I know? And why do you suddenly want to know, anyhow?"

"Well," observed the child, "grandpa got off there."

GRANDMA: How did Dennis do on his history exam?

MOTHER: Oh, not at all well. But it wasn't his fault. Why, they asked him about things that happened before he was born!

Shirtliff hated to fly so he took the long train ride from Chicago to Seattle. His wife of 43 years met him at the station. Shirtliff staggered off the train. "It's terrible riding backwards for hours on end," he complained. "I never could stand that."

"Why," asked his wife, "didn't you ask the person sitting opposite to change seats with you?"

"Couldn't," he said. "There wasn't anybody there."

"Is Milicent truthful about how old she is?"

"My wife never lies about her age. She just tells people she's as old as I am. Then she lies about *my* age!"

Hilliard, 79, complained to his eye doctor of seeing dark spots in front of his eyes.

"Well, I think glasses will help," said the doctor. He wrote out a prescription.

Hilliard reported back to the doctor a week later. "Do the glasses help?" the M.D. asked.

"Oh, yeah, they really do," said the old man. "I can see the spots much more clearly now."

In a small Mississippi town, Clapton, a con man, was selling a magic elixir guaranteed to make people live forever. "Take a good look at me," Clapton said to the crowd of older people gathered outside of the supermarket. "Feast your eyes on a man who is two hundred and fifty years old."

Caruthers walked over to the con man's young assistant and asked, "Is he really that old?"

"I don't know," the assistant replied, "I've only been working for him for seventy-five years."

Grandpa McAdoo lay in bed very close to death. His children and grandchildren stood in the living room waiting for the end. He beckoned to Kevin, the youngest grandson, who peeked into the bedroom for a last look at the old man.

"What's that I smell coming from the kitchen?" the dying man asked his grandson.

"Grandma's making some corned beef and cabbage," said the youngster.

"Go ask her if I could have a little piece," said the man.

The youngster returned in a moment and announced, "Grandma says you can't have any. It's for the wake!"

Clifford, aged 10, and his grandparents, Martha and Horace, were sitting in a cocktail lounge in a train station when they heard a whistle. The three of them rushed out of the bar onto the platform only to discover that they'd missed the train.

"The next train is in one hour," said the stationmaster.

The three went back into the lounge. Martha and Horace had another drink. Clifford had a Coke. They heard a whistle, rushed out and discovered the train pulling away.

"Next one is sixty minutes from now!" said the perplexed stationmaster.

An hour later, Clifford, with his grandma and grandpa, raced out onto the platform, and his grandparents leaped onto the train as it pulled away. The boy was left standing on the platform and began to laugh uproariously.

"Your grandparents just left you," said the stationmaster. "Why are you laughing?"

"They came to see me off!"

Owens, 94, and Beck, 88, were the two oldest residents of a retirement home in Philadelphia. The doctors and staff believed both men only continued to live so they could roast each other.

After lunch the two men sat on the porch.

"Once I had a beard like yours," said Owens, "and when I saw how lousy I looked, I cut it off."

"I used to have a face like yours too," said Beck, "and when I saw how lousy it made me look, I grew a beard."

CHAPERONE

One who could never make the team
but is still in there intercepting passes.

There was an old couple from Rayville
Whose habits were quite medieval
    They would strip to the skin
    Then each take a pin
And pick lint from the other one's navel.

Piedmont was telling buddies about unintentionally driving through a puddle of water and splashing an old codger visiting from Florida.

"How'd you know he was from Florida?" asked one co-worker. "Did you stop to apologize?"

"No," replied Piedmont. "I didn't stop because he was awfully big and he looked mad. But I knew he was from Florida because I could hear him yelling something about the sun and the beach."

**There's only one thing
wrong with going through a second
childhood. You can't blame your parents!**

Mrs. Jensen woke up at three a.m. in the retirement home, called her youngest son on the phone and wished him a happy birthday.

"Gee, Mom, is there anything wrong?" asked the son.

"Why, no. It's your fiftieth birthday, so I thought I'd call you."

"Good grief, Mother, you didn't drag me out of bed at three o'clock in the morning just to wish me a happy birthday, did you?"

"Well son, fifty years ago tonight you made me get up at three a.m. and now I'm paying you back."

Chalmers ran into an old maid at the town drugstore and said, "Emily, I hear you're getting married."

"That is absolutely not true," she answered, "but thank God for the rumor."

In Sun City, Mrs. Lowe, 78, brought, Kipp, her former boyfriend, into court, claiming he'd stolen her furniture.

"I didn't do it!" cried the defendant. "She gave me all that junk, and money too."

"Why would she do that?" asked the white-haired judge.

"Why, for the use of my body," replied the old fellow. "What else?"

"Don't listen, your honor!" shouted Mrs. Lowe. "He's even older than you are. He must be taking pills to say such crazy things!"

"Just how old are you, mister?" asked the judge.

"I am eighty-nine," answered Kipp proudly, "and still plugging away!"

"Don't listen!" yelled Mrs. Lowe. "He's on pills ..."

"Please be silent, madam!" demanded the elderly judge. "I'm trying to find out what kind of pills he's on!"

There are so many retirement communities in Florida the natives are now calling their state "God's waiting room."

Two old maids were reading the paper when one of them spied an article of special interest. In the obituary column was a notice that a woman's third husband had died and would be cremated in the morning. One of the old maids said, "It's not fair. We can't get one, and some women have husbands to burn!"

OLD MAIDS

Girls who talk about boy-gone days.

Did you hear about the old maid who found a burglar under her bed?

She called the police and insisted they send someone over in the morning.

Bud and Oscar were chatting at the old folks home about their friend Otto.

"Well, after five years of chasing that young chorus girl, he finally got hitched to her," said Bud.

"He had to marry her," said Oscar, "for his money."

PHYLLIS: Tell me, dear, what do you think of sex?
SHEILA: I think it's the finest department store
in New York!

An old geezer grabbed Gordeen's sleeve during a fashion show and said, "Here I am at seventy-five and when I look at those models I wish I was twenty years older."

"You mean twenty years younger, don't you?"

"No, I mean twenty years older — then I wouldn't give a damn about them."

Eighty-two-year-old Hanson was recovering nicely in a private hospital. Each day he pinched the nurse's behind and made lewd remarks.

"With your mind," the young nurse scolded, "you should be living in a bordello."

"At these prices," said Hanson, "I could afford to."

Tillie and Rebecca were passing the time of day in the garden of a Portola Valley retirement home.

"My grandson is taking nuclear physics," said Tillie.

"As far as I'm concerned," said Rebecca, "Milk of Magnesia is plenty strong enough."

"Why are you lookin' at me like that?" asked Burl.

"I'm trying to figure out one of the great mysteries of life," replied Horace.

"What's that?"

"How can that idiot who married your daughter be the father of the smartest grandchildren in the world?"

Did you hear about the grandfather of 92 who married a woman of 84?

They spent their entire honeymoon getting out of the car.

Barrett and Strobe were walking through Griffith Park when suddenly it began to rain heavily.

"Open your umbrella!" said Barrett.

"My umbrella ain't worth a damn," said Strobe. "It's full of holes."

"Holes? Then why did you bring it?"

"Did I know it was gonna rain?"

When Morgan reached the age of sixty-five, he suddenly began chasing the young chicks. A neighbor brought his behavior to the attention of his wife. "Whatta you gonna do about it?" she asked.

"Who cares?" said Mrs. Morgan. "Let him go ahead and chase girls! Dogs chase cars — but when they catch them, they can't drive!"

Professor Waterhouse was going to Africa on a research trip and put a classified ad in the newspaper:

> Wanted: A man who can speak at least five languages, loves to travel and knows how to use a gun.

The next day, Kerrigan, 78, applied. "Do you love to travel?" asked Waterhouse.

"Me?" said Kerrigan, "I hate traveling. Boats make me seasick, planes I wouldn't get on, and trains are the worst of them all."

"But you are a linguist," continued the professor. "I presume you speak Urdu, Arabic, Greek —"

"What?" interrupted the old man. "I know a little Gaelic. That's all."

"Well, can you use firearms?" persisted the professor.

"No, I'm afraid a guns."

"Then what the devil did you come here for?"

"I saw your ad," said Kerrigan, "and I just came to tell you that you better not count on me."

An old-timer is anyone who remembers when the air was clean and sex was dirty.

DRINKING DILLIES

**Some men would live strictly on a
liquid diet if it weren't for pretzels and peanuts.**

McGinty was steering for a saloon when a Protestant
minister stopped him. "My man, don't go into that saloon!
Don't you know that the Devil is with you?"

"I didn't recognize you, your Reverence," said McGinty,
"but Devil or not, come on anyhow — I'm settin' up the pair
of us."

Old Mrs. Kerrigan came back from a Caribbean cruise
with more than her five-bottle liquor allotment. She thought
she'd hide it from customs by pouring two fifths of gin into
a large jar.

When the ship docked, the customs inspector looked at
the jar suspiciously and asked, "What do you have in there?"

"Oh," said the Irish woman, "that's holy water."

The inspector opened the jar, tasted the contents and
exclaimed, "Holy water, nothing! That's gin!"

"Glory be!" cried Mrs. Kerrigan, "another miracle!"

"Every time I see you," screamed Howell's wife, "you've got a bottle in your pocket!"

"You don't expect me to keep it in me mouth all the time, do you?" replied her husband.

KILLARNEY COCKTAIL

Two sips and you turn green!

Monahan stumbled into a saloon half crocked. "Hey," he said to the bartender, "how tall is a penguin?"

"About two and a half feet!"

"Thank God!" he sobbed. "I thought I ran over a nun!"

Comedian Jackie Gleason is said to have stepped up to a Miami Beach bar and asked for a martini consisting of 24 parts gin and 1 part vermouth.

"Coming up!" said the bewildered bartender. "Want a twist of lemon peel in it?"

"Look, buddy," snapped Gleason, "if I want a lemonade, I'll ask for it!"

"I'm sorry to tell you this, Ma'am," the foreman announced at Mrs Hotchkis's doorstep, "but your husband drowned in a vat of beer down at the brewery!"

"Oh, the poor man!" cried the woman. "He didn't stand a chance!"

"Yes, he did! He got out twice to take a leak!"

Burton stumbled into the house to the amazement of his wife. "What happened?" she asked. "You've never come home drunk before. How'd you get this way?"

"Two Scotsmen ruined me," declared Burton.

"Who were they?"

"Haig and Haig!"

Drinking Dillies

How can you tell when an Irish patient is recovering?
He tries to blow the foam off his medicine!

Peabody was married to an old shrew who nagged him
all the time. In desperation he began drinking and every
night came home smashed. Hoping to cure him, Mrs.
Peabody went to her neighbor, Mrs. Quinn, and asked for
some advice.

"The thing to do," suggested Mrs. Quinn, "is to scare
him to death. When he comes home at night, he takes a short
cut through the cemetery. Scare the bejezus out of him, and
he'll never drink again."

So Mrs. Peabody rented a devil's costume and hid
behind a tombstone in the cemetery. That night as Peabody
stumbled by, she jumped out and growled, "Ahh, ah, ah!"

"Who are you?" slobbered Peabody.

"I am the Devil!"

"Shake hands, I'm married to your sister!"

TOOHEY'S TOAST

At last I've found the perfect girl,
I could not ask for more;
She's deaf and dumb and oversexed
And she owns a liquor store.

Kully and Lane were having a few at a new tavern in
town. After an hour of heavy imbibing Kully asked the
bartender where the washroom was.

"Go to the door, left of the elevator," said the barkeep,
"then walk down two steps and there you are."

Kully forgot to turn left. He opened the elevator door,
took one step and fell down the shaft.

Ten minutes later, Lane followed Kully and saw him
lying on the bottom of the shaft.

"Look out for that second step," shouted up Kully, "it's
a real bitch!"

177

"Did you see how Dumbrowski came to work today?"
"No."
"I tell ya the man was so loaded they made him use the freight elevator!"

Rollie and Jasper were strolling through a cow pasture. "At mah funeral," said Rollie, "Ah want yew to pour a jug a corn likker over mah grave."

"Ah'll be glad to," said Jasper. "But would yew mind if it passes through mah kidneys first?"

The tender young love of a beautiful girl
And the love of a strong young man,
And the love of a mother for her child
Have gone on since time began;
But the greatest love, the love of love,
Even greater than that of a mother,
Is the all-consuming, infinite love
Of one drunken bum for another.

Father Aragon was at a pitch of fervor in his sermon on drinking. "What could be worse than drink?" he boomed.
"Thirst!" shouted Gomez from the rear.

"Me mother-in-law's gone to her final reward," said Brannigan to the bartender in Taggert's Tavern, "and it's a twenty spot that I'm needin' for a wreath. Could you be advancin' me the twenty?"

The bartender emptied his pockets and the cash register but the total came to only $15.30.

"That'll do," said Brannigan quickly. "I'll take the other $4.70 in drinks!"

Drinking Dillies

Riddock was staggering up the street from telephone pole to lamp post and back again. Father Duncan stopped him and said, "Drunk again!"

"Are you?" said Riddock. "So'm I Father!"

"This is no time for levity!" admonished the priest. "After taking the pledge and promising me two weeks ago you'd never drink again — it's a sin against God and the Church and I'm sorry to be saying so!"

"You're sorry to see me so?"

"Indeed, I am!"

"Are you sure you're sorry?"

"Yes, very, very sorry!"

"Then if you're really, really sorry," said Riddock, "I'll forgive you, Father!"

Eckert, visiting friends in Nashville, had returned to his hotel after a night of celebrating. He wobbled up to the desk clerk and said, "Give me the key to room 712!"

Five minutes later, Eckert lurched up to the desk again. "Give me the key to room 712!"

"Hey, what's going on?" asked the clerk. "I just gave the key to 712 to some guy!"

"That was me! I fell out of the window!"

When elderly Lockridge collapsed on the street, a crowd soon gathered and began making suggestions as to how the old fellow should be revived.

Rosalee Murdock shouted, "Why don't you give the poor man some whiskey!"

No one paid any attention to her. Finally, Lockridge opened one eye, pulled himself up on an elbow and said weakly, "Will the lot of you hold your tongues and let dear Rosalee Murdock speak!"

**Ice is a great healer,
especially when used in a glass of vodka!**

Milbank, cockeyed drunk, noticed a man coming out of a supermarket carrying two big bags of groceries.

"Look at him spending all that money for food," he said to no one in particular. "I bet he ain't got a drop of liquor in the house!"

REDNECK LULLABY

Empty The Beer Barrel Slowly,
Mamma, Pappy's Been Missing for Days.

Bracken and Colefax shuffled into an establishment for the thirsty and leaned on the bar. Bracken ordered a triple whiskey, swallowed it in one gulp, then swirled around and fell face down flat onto the sawdust floor.

"That's what I like about Bracken," said the bartender to Colefax. "He always knows when he's had enough."

The train for New York had just pulled out of Washington. The passengers were all settling back in their seats comfortably, when a tall, dignified gentleman entered the club car.

"I beg your pardon," he queried, "is there by chance, an Irishman here?"

"I'm Irish," shouted McQuinlan, standing up proudly.

"Oh, that's wonderful!" boomed the man. "Could I be borrowin' your cockscrew?"

In London one evening, Comstock and Marsh reeled out of a pub and climbed on a double-decker bus. Comstock insisted on going up topside. After a short time upstairs, he came lurching down to his pal, white as a sheet.

"What's wrong?" asked Marsh.

"Don't dare go upstairs!" sputtered Comstock. "There's no driver!"

Drinking Dillies

"Prisoner, why did you knock down, beat up and kick this man so shamefully?"

"I'm very sorry for that, your Honor! It was all a mistake. I was a little under the weather and I thought he was my wife!"

Inebriated old Kincaid, swaying unsteadily and his arms flailing wildly, flagged down a bus on the corner.

"Driver," he cried when the door was opened for him, "do you go to Forty-shecon' Shtreet?"

"Yes, I do," said the driver.

"An' Broadway?"

"That's right, Forty-second and Broadway."

"Well, g'bye," waved the juiced-up New Yorker, "and have a good time!"

"Didja hear the news?" asked Cunningham of his pal at the neighborhood saloon. "Decker drank so much his wife left him!"

"Waiter! Give me six boilermakers!"

"I notice Leonid doesn't wear glasses any longer!"

"It's true! He read so much about the evils of drinking vodka that he gave up reading!"

Flynn was carrying a bottle of scotch in his hip pocket while marching in the St. Paddy's Day Parade. He staggered down one of the side streets and was immediately hit by a truck. As he lay on the ground, Flynn felt the wetness in his pants, and looked up at the sky. "Oh, Father in heaven," he cried, "please let it be blood!"

"Novelli does other things beside drink!"
"What?"
"He hiccups!"

Boozed-up Beacham bobbed up to a man on the street and bummed a nickel from him. He walked over to a mail box, opened it, dropped the nickel in the slot and then looked up at the clock on a nearby building.

"I'll be damned!" slobbered Beacham. "I've lost ten pounds and I just weighed myself last night!"

"Why do you drink?" asked Cinelli.

"Booze killed me mother," answered Finnerty, "booze killed me father. I'm drinkin' for revenge!"

A preacher walked into a San Diego saloon and ordered tequila. The bartender put the glass on the bar. "I'm going to show you the evils of drink!" said the preacher. Whereupon he pulled a worm out of his pocket and dropped it in the glass. In a few seconds, the worm was dead.

"There," said the preacher to Gonzales who was draped over the bar. "Has that taught you a lesson?"

"Yeah, it sure has," said Gonzales. "If you have worms, drink tequila!"

Garvey's hair kept falling out and he complained to his barber. "That stuff you gave me is terrible!" he cried. "You said two bottles of it would really make my hair grow but nothing's happened."

"I don't understand it," said the barber. "That's the best hair restorer made."

"Well," said Garvey. "I don't mind drinking another bottle, but it better work this time."

Drinking Dillies

Clay celebrated New Year's Eve so well he woke up the next day in the hospital. His friend Mapes came to visit him.

"What happened last night?" asked Clay.

"You had quite a load on," answered Mapes. "You walked over to the window, climbed out on the sill and announced to the world that you were going to fly all over the borough of Manhattan!"

"My God! " shouted Clay. "Why didn't you stop me?"

"Tell you the truth," replied Mapes, "last night, I really thought you could do it!"

"Drinkin' doesn't affect me at all," bragged Bussey. "Last night, I was boozin' it up all night long and I was in great shape. The only trouble was that people kept steppin' on my fingers!"

"Didn't you tell me Jenkins joined AA?"

"I did!"

"Then, what happened?"

"He never went to the meetings. He used to drink and then send in the bottles."

"I had a dream the other night," said Duncan to his pal MacPherson, "and it taught me a great lesson."

"What was it?" asked MacPherson.

"I dreamed I was in Rome and I had an audience with the Pope. 'Would I have a drink?' he asked me. Thinks I, 'would a duck swim?' And seeing the whiskey and lemons and sugar on the sideboard, I told him I wouldn't mind a drop of punch. 'Cold or hot?' he asked me. 'Hot, your Holiness,' said I. An' that's where I made my mistake!"

"I don't see anything wrong —."

"His Holiness stepped toward the kitchen to boil the water and before he got back, I woke up!"

"What lesson did you learn?" asked MacPherson.

"Next time," swore Duncan, "I'll say, 'I'll take it cold, your Holiness, while the water's gettin' hot!'"

"I hear Mr. Grady up in apartment 6F is quite a lush."

"Well, Grady calls himself a nutritional drinker. He starts off each day with the juice from three martinis."

TOOLEY'S TOAST

Here's to our bartender —
may he never be low in spirits.

McAdoo was getting blotto at the Berrigan wake. After an hour he tip-toed up to the hostess and said, "Do lemons have legs?"

"Lemons with legs?" exclaimed Mrs. Berrigan. "You must be losin' your mind!"

"In that case," said McAdoo, "I'm afraid I've just squeezed your canary into me whiskey!"

"Would you say that Chickering drinks quite a bit?"

"I'm not sure. He says he drinks just to steady himself!"

"Is that right? Well, last night he got so steady he couldn't move!"

Carlson and Berby had been at a bar, putting away brews for over two hours. "I have to go!" said Carlson, motioning toward the men's room.

"Go ahead!" said Berby.

Five minutes later, Carlson returned. "Did you go for me?" asked Berby.

"No!" answered his friend, who turned around and headed back to the washroom.

When he returned, Carlson said, "Aw, you didn't have to go!"

Drinking Dillies

Moody and Kelm saw a man siphoning gas from a car. Moody said to his friend, "I hope I never get that thirsty!"

Mrs. Vandercook, the temperance lecturer, pounded the lectern as she warned the audience about the evils of booze.

"Who is the richest man in town?" she shouted. "Who has the biggest house? The saloon keeper! And who pays for it all? You do, my friends, you do!"

A few days later, Hoffmeyer, who had been in the audience, met Mrs. Vandercook on the street and congratulated her on the effectiveness of her speech.

"I'm glad to see that you've given up drinking," said the temperance lecturer.

"Well, not exactly," said Hoffmeyer, "I just went and bought a saloon."

"I've been drinkin' whiskey all week long ta cure mah sciatica," admitted Billy Bob.

"Ah ken give yew a cure."

"Shut up. Ah don't wanna hear it."

Hogeland sneaked into the bedroom and started making love to his sleeping wife till she awakened and shouted, "Is that you?"

"It better be!" snorted Hogeland.

"When're you gonna stop this sinnin'?" she demanded. "Moody quit smokin'. Payne stopped gamblin'. What're you gonna give up?"

"Okay," slurred Hoagland through bloodshot eyes, "from now on, you sleep in the bedroom and I'll sleep in the spare room."

Three weeks went by with Mrs. Hogeland sleeping alone. Finally, unable to contain herself for one more night, she tiptoed to the spare room and tapped lightly on the door. "All right, what is it?" shouted Hogeland.

"I just wanted to tell ya," said his wife sweetly, "that Moody is smokin' again!"

For a holiday, Langston decided to go to Switzerland and climb the Matterhorn. He hired a guide and just as they neared the top, the men were caught in a snow slide.

Three hours later, a Saint Bernard plowed through to them, a keg of brandy tied under his chin. "Hooray!" shouted the guide. "Here comes man's best friend!"

"Yeah," said Langston. "An' look at the size of the dog that's bringin' it!"

"Ah got me a money problem which is causin' me drink problems," said Luster.

"Why's that?" asked Elgart.

"Ah just never have me enough money ta buy all Ah wanna drink."

Following the presentation of evidence against a Kentucky moonshiner, the judge asked the jury, "Do any of you have any questions that you would like to ask of the defendant, before you consider the evidence?"

"Yes, yore honor," said the jury foreman, "a couple of us would like ta know how long the defendant boils the malt, and what is the best way ta keep the yeast out?"

SALESMAN: I have something here that'll make you feel like a new man, bring new friendship and popularity into your life, and...

THETCHEL: Never mind the rest, ah'll take a quart.

Mrs. Kirgan was arguing with her daughter Tina. "It's a shame, that husband of yours," she exclaimed. "Never been seen without a bottle in his mouth!"

"That's not true, mama!" protested Tina in her husband's defense. "Sometimes David stops drinking."

"To do what?" asked her mother.

"Well, to belch, for one!" replied Tina.

Drinking Dillies

Manley was brought into night court, not just for being drunk but also on suspicion that he was the notorious night prowler. "All right, what were you doing out at 3 a.m.?" asked the judge.

"I was going to a lecture."

"A lecture at three in the morning?" asked the judge.

"Oh, sure," said Manley. "Some timesh my wife shtaysh up longer than that."

Chernik was blotto and stumbling along Woodward Avenue at 4:30 in the morning, panic stricken. A cop stopped him and said, "Do you have an explanation?"

"If I have explanation, mister policeman," slobbered Chernik, "I be home with my wife!"

"Yew wanna know why Ah come home loaded?" sputtered the drunken Virgil.

"Yes," said his wife.

"Because Ah run out a money, that's why."

It was Ryan's 104th birthday. Reporters gathered around him and one of them asked the routine question, "Please, tell us, sir, to what do you attribute your long life?"

"I have never touched a drop of intoxicating liquor!" answered the old man.

Suddenly, from the next room, there came a tremendous crash, followed by a barrage of angry shouts.

"Good Heavens, what was that?" cried the reporter.

"Oh," explained Ryan, "that's my father. He always makes a lot of noise when he's drunk!"

**There is one basic difference
between a drunk and an alcoholic —
the drunk doesn't have to go to meetings.**

187

Lenox and Hays were sitting on a Charleston curb in the wee small hours of the night.

"What's your wife shay when you shtay out thish late?" asked Lenox.

"Haven't got a wife," said Hays.

"Then what's the idea of shtayin' out sho late?"

Gannon and Hayward finished off three fifths of whiskey one afternoon and found themselves on the roller coaster at Coney Island. Gannon said, "We're making good time, but I'm not sure this is the right bus."

Machlin stumbled into the house around four in the morning. He was only half drunk, partly dressed, smeared with lipstick and smelling of cheap perfume. "Hello, darlin'," said Macklin to his wife.

"How dare you," screamed Mrs. Macklin, "come home in that condition when we're goin' to a funeral tomorrow?"

"A funeral," said Macklin. "Whose?"

"Yours," she replied.

"I'm against liquor. It caused my father's death."

"Drank too much?"

"No, a case fell on his head."

In Chicago, a policeman strolling his early morning beat, stopped in front of a house. Sitting there on the steps was old man Blake, completely snookered.

"Why don't you go on home?" suggested the cop.

"I live here!" said Blake.

"Why don't you go inside then?"

"I lost my key," answered the drunk.

"Why don't you ring the bell?"

"I did .... an hour ago!"

"Why don't you ring it again?" asked the officer.

"The hell with 'em," snorted Blake, "let 'em wait!"

Drinking Dillies

"Mah cousin Zeke just fell down the stairs with a quart a Kentucky bourbon and didn't spill a single drop!"
"How's that possible?"
"He kept his mouth closed!"

Bryant, the bartender, loved boxing. Two customers got him talking about Mohammed Ali and his great fights. Meantime, they kept ordering drinks and each time Bryant tried to collect, one of the men said, "Eh, you rang it up!"

After the two cheaters left, Hambrick, who had been watching their trick, tried the same thing. "Now hold on!" said the bartender. "Don't you be givin' me any of that boxing routine!"

"What boxing? What routine?" asked Hambrick. "Just give me my change and let me out of here!"

Rizzutti was sitting in the neighborhood bar. Next to him sat Fyler who had had more than enough beer and was staring at his empty glass. He turned to Rizzutti and asked, "Shay, did you shpill a glash of beer on me?"

"Absolutely, not!" Rizzutti replied.

Fyler turned to the man on his other side. "Mishter, did you by any chance throw a glash of beer in my lap?"

"No!" snapped the man.

"Jusht what I been sushpectin'," Fyler slobbered. "It'sh an inside job!"

Hawkins climbed off his stool at the bar and dragged himself into the men's room. Suddenly he began howling and the bartender came racing in.

"Every time I flush this damn thing," stammered Hawkins, "it bites me!"

"Of course it does," said the bartender. "You're sitting on the mop bucket."

Most of the time, two pints will make a cavort!

The owner of a bar was awakened at 4 a.m. by a phone call. "Hey, mister," said a voice. "When does your saloon open in the mornin'?"

"Sorry, you can't get in till noon."

"I don't want to get in — I want to get out!"

Crawford, Dickerson and Greer had been drinking buddies for thirty-five years. Crawford passed away and the other two went to visit him late one night at the funeral parlor. "Don't you think we ought to take him out for one last drink?" asked Dickerson.

"I do," agreed Greer.

They picked him up out of the coffin, carried him to a saloon and leaned him up against the bar. They asked for three scotches and drank them all. They ordered three more. Then three more. Three more ... three more ...

Finally the bartender said, "Okay guys, I'm closing up, that'll be 86 bucks."

"All right," said Dickerson, "our buddy here will take care of the check!" And they walked out.

The bartender walked over to the dead Crawford and said, "That'll be 86 bucks!"

No answer.

"Listen fella, I'm closin' up and I gotta have 86 bucks."

No answer.

"Look buddy, you don't give me the 86 bucks I'm gonna put this fist through your mouth."

Pow! He hit Crawford and the body fell to the floor.

At that moment Dickerson and Greer come running back in. "Holy mackerel!" screamed Greer, "you've killed our best friend."

The bartender said, "I had to. He pulled a knife on me!"

GAMBLING GIGGLES

**An habitual gambler never gives up and
never gives in, even when his money gives out.**

Did you hear about the New Yorker who just came back
from three glorious weeks in Las Vegas where he underwent
a rather unusual operation?

He had his wallet removed and they didn't even give him
an anesthetic.

Tiernan was talking to his son as he lay on his deathbed.
"Son, promise me you'll never play blackjack. It's a game
that'll cost you a fortune, waste your time, ruin your health
and cause you endless hours of anguish and pain. Do you
promise me, here on my dying bed, with the merciful angel
of death hovering about and almighty God as a witness, that
you'll never play blackjack?"

"Yes, Pop," muttered the son.

"And remember," shouted Tiernan, "if you must play
always be sure to take the bank."

Stobart prayed every night for divine intervention to help him win the lottery. Night after night he sent his pleas on high without results. "Lord, please let me win the lottery," begged Stobart. "Give me a break!"

Then suddenly through a roll of thunder and flashes of lightning there came a booming voice from above: "You give ME a break! Buy a ticket!"

Finkelstein was showered with congratulations when his number 56 won first prize in the lottery.

His steam room buddy Berkowitz asked him, "How in the world did you happen to pick number 56?"

"It was easy," said Finkelstein. "I saw it in a dream. Nine 8's appeared and jumped before my eyes. Nine times 8 is 56. That's all there was to it."

"Wait a minute, my friend," protested Berkowitz. "Nine times 8 is not 56!"

"All right, all right," snapped the new millionaire. "You be the mathematician."

A big-time gambler was dead and the funeral oration was in progress. The church was filled with the gambler's professional cronies. The minister concluded the service by saying, "Deuces McCluskey isn't dead, he only sleeps!"

From the back of the chapel came a raspy voice, "Hey, I got 5 G's says he don't wake up."

Lavinia, a hatchet-faced old biddy, tapped the keeper of the monkey house indignantly on the shoulder.

"Those wretched animals of yours are engaged in shooting dice. I demand that you go in there and break up the game at once."

"I'm sorry but those monkeys are keeping strictly within the law, ma'am," sighed the keeper. "They're only playing for peanuts."

Gambling Giggles

Chandler and Rouse, patients in a hospital ward, became bored. They found a stack of diagnosis cards in a corner and began a game of poker. Chandler shuffled the cards and dealt. They picked up their hands and looked at the cards. Chandler bet, Rouse raised, then each man raised and raised again until Chandler finally called.

"Looks like I win, buddy. I've got three pneumonias and two gallstones."

"Hold on, not so fast. I've got four enemas."

"Well, I guess you take the pot."

Snakes, a cheating gambler, was in a hot back barroom game of craps. The pot was enormous. Snakes shook the dice, rolled and as bad luck would have it, a third die slipped out of his sleeve and fell on the table with the other two.

No one said a word. Muggsy Mulligan, the toughest guy in the city, picked up the third die, slipped it into his pocket and handed Snakes the other two. "Roll 'em," said Muggsy. "Your point is fifteen."

Did you hear about the department store in Las Vegas that hired a Santa Claus?

The kids tell him what they want and he gives them the odds on getting it.

Kelsey and Seaton were chatting during a company coffee break. "I had a great dream last night," said Kelsey. "I dreamed I won $20,000,000 in Atlantic City."

"I had a great dream too," said Seaton. "I dreamed I was in a room with Madonna and Melanie Griffith."

"Wow! Melanie and Madonna. Why didn't you call me?"

"I did, but your wife said you were in Atlantic City!"

The trouble with hitting the jackpot on a slot machine is that it takes so long to put the money back in the machine.

If you're a Reno resident you've got to keep your eyes open at all times. A woman there stepped out of a little neighborhood laundromat for less than five minutes — and somebody won her wash.

KIBITZER

A person who'll bet your
shirt on somebody else's hand.

Harmon, a homeless panhandler, stopped VanSloan, a well-dressed stockbroker, on San Francisco's Union Square and asked for 50 cents for a little food.

"I haven't got any change," said VanSloan, "but I'll buy you a drink."

"I don't drink," said Harmon. "Honest, all I want is a half a buck for a little chow."

"I'll buy you a cigar," offered the stockbroker.

"All I want, mister, is a little food," said Harmon. "I don't smoke, honest."

"Okay, I'll put some cash down on a horse for you."

"Mister, I never gamble," said the panhandler. "I want something to eat, that's all."

"All right, you come home with me for dinner," said VanSloan. "I want my wife to see what happens to a guy who doesn't drink, smoke or gamble."

Judge Whitby glared down at the defendant.

"Fuzzy Chetwode," rasped the justice, "you are charged with assault and battery, and with mutilating the plaintiff by biting off a piece of his nose. How do you plead?"

"I plead innocent, your Honor," blared Chetwode. "There was five of us in that poker game and all of us got into the fight. Why, it coulda been any one of us who bit off his nose."

"No, it couldn't," retorted the judge. "The injured man saw you spit it out!"

Gambling Giggles

Lucky and Studs were inveterate gamblers and each weekend found them together at the local club where they played pinochle all night.

"Why the long face?" asked Lucky as they sat down for their usual game.

"It's my wife," mourned Studs. "She gave me final warning that if I didn't give up cards she'd leave me."

"Hey, that's terrible," replied Lucky. "I really sympathize with you."

"Yeah, thanks," muttered Studs. "I'm sure gonna miss the old gal."

Tamaline was telling his pal Asher about his plans for the camping trip he was going on.

"Got a map? A compass?" asked Asher.

"Of course," said Tamaline.

"How about a deck of cards?"

"What am I going to do with a deck of cards?"

"A deck of cards might save your life," said Asher. "Listen, suppose you get lost. All you have to do is sit down and open the deck and start to play solitaire. The next thing you know some idiot will pop up behind you and start telling you what card to play next."

Spengler, a spiritualist who loved poker, wanted another player for a Saturday night session and summoned the ghost of a departed companion. The ghost was delighted to sit in on the game, and on the very first hand drew five beautiful hearts. He bet his stack.

Unfortunately, McKelvey, one of the real flesh-and-blood players, had a pat full house and raked in the pot — just one more time when the spirit was willing but the flush was weak.

**A gambler doesn't always know
where his dollar is coming from —
but he always knows where it's going to.**

Miss Piecroft, the kindergarten teacher, called her class to attention and asked, "Who would like to tell us how to count today?"

Gareth, a gambler's 7-year-old son, stood up and recited, "1,2,3,4,5,6,7,8,9,10, jack, queen, king."

Have you heard about the new literature club for gamblers?

They are calling it the Bookie of the Month.

Dr. Foxworth, the famous psychologist, had finished his lecture and was answering questions.

Seely, a meek little man, asked, "Did you say that a good poker player could hold down any kind of executive job?"

"That's right," answered the shrink. "Does that raise a question in your mind?"

"Yes," said Seely. "What would a good poker player want with a job?"

Sir Percival Snyde-Smith, on a visit to Chicago, got mixed up in a poker game with some strangers. By chance he happened to win a big pot. One of the players congratulated him with, "Lucky dog!"

"Are you insulting me?" asked the Englishman.

"Why, no," said the American. "That's a term of congratulation with us, and the right thing to say on an occasion like this."

Back in England, Sir Percival was playing bridge with his host and hostess and another guest at a country house party. His hostess bid and made a grand slam, and as she raked in the stakes Snyde-Smith leaned over to her and smiled, "Lucky bitch!"

Card playing can be expensive — but so can any game where you begin by holding hands.

Gambling Giggles

Why is a man who never bets as bad as a gambler?
Because he is no better.

LAS VEGAS

A great place to go to get
tanned and faded at the same time.

Smethurst and Burkett, two big bucks industrialists,
were seated in their club having a friendly argument.

"I tell you there's a shirt shop on 68th street between
Park and Madison," said Smethurst.

"I say there isn't," challenged Burkett. "How about a
sociable bet on it. Say one million dollars."

"Okay, and a box of cigars," agreed Smethurst. "Let's
make it interesting."

Last night I held a little hand
So dainty and so sweet,
I thought my heart would surely break
So wildly it did beat;
No other hand in all the world
Can greater solace bring,
Than the pretty hand I held last night,
Four Aces and a King!

"The people in my little town have to go to the city to get
married," said Waddle.

"Don't you have a clergyman?" asked his friend Daniel.

"Our minister is so strict he won't even perform a
wedding ceremony," said Waddle.

"Why?" asked Daniel. "What in heaven's name has that
got to do with morals?"

"He says his conscience will not let him take part in any
game of chance."

Greenblatt, an inveterate gambler, left the Las Vegas dice table and wired his partner in New York: "Having a wonderful time — wish I could afford it."

GIN RUMMY

A card game in which a good
deal depends on a good deal.

The youngster fidgeted and turned with imploring eyes toward his father. "Why can't I go out and play football or baseball or basketball like the other boys?"

The father slapped his fist down on the table and shouted, "Shut up and deal!"

Drew and Jill shared a passionate love of gambling and went to Atlantic City for their honeymoon. For nearly a week they were dogged by bad luck. On the morning of their final day they had only two dollars left between them.

"Let me go out to the track alone today, honey," pleaded Drew. "Wait for me at the hotel. I've got a hunch."

At the track, Drew picked a 50-to-1 shot on the first race and won. Every succeeding race was captured by a long shot and Drew was backing it every time. At the end of the afternoon he had over $18,000.

On the way back to the hotel, he decided to cash in further on his lucky streak, and stopped in one of the casinos. His luck held. He ran his stake up to $60,000. Drew was just about to leave when the roulette wheel began spinning once more. Suddenly he took a deep breath and put the entire $60,000 on black.

The ball bounced, and settled. "Number fourteen," called the croupier. "Red."

Drew walked back to the hotel. Jill was waiting for him in the lobby.

"How did you make out?" she called eagerly.

"I lost the two dollars," said Drew.

Gambling Giggles

Why is Las Vegas known as the most religious city in the world?

Because any time you walk into a casino you can hear someone say, "Oh, my God!"

"How would *you* have played that hand," demanded a losing pinochle player.

The kibitzer replied, "Under an assumed name."

A physicist had a horseshoe hanging on the door of his laboratory. His colleagues were surprised and asked whether he believed it would bring luck to his experiments.

He answered, "No, I don't believe in superstitions. But I have been told that it works even if you don't believe in it!"

When Chance and Jenni were at Bally's in Reno he gave her a hundred dollars to squander at roulette.

"What number shall I play?" she asked.

"What's the difference?" said Chance. "It's pure luck. Try the number that corresponds with your age."

So, she plunked down the hundred dollar bill on 29. The little ball whirled around and landed on 38. Jenni fainted.

In a "friendly" poker game, Dr. Bebb, the town's leading M.D., was losing badly. Suddenly a hand of stud came along in which he finally drew aces back to back. Furthermore, everybody stayed. On the next turn of the cards, Dr. Bebb drew another ace! Unfortunately, at that moment, his friend Kyle, sitting at his right, had a heart attack, slumped over the table and breathed his last.

The white-faced players carried him to a couch. "What'll we do now?" they implored the physician.

"Out of respect for the dead, I suggest we finish this hand standing up."

Nesbitt, a henpecked husband, was winning big in a game with the guys from the garage. He didn't like to quit when he was so far ahead, but as the hours went by, he grew visibly more apprehensive. Flora was going to kill him. Suddenly at about 3 a.m. he had an inspiration. He called his wife on the phone and when Flora answered, he cried to her, "Don't pay the ransom, darling, I've escaped."

"Did you read where the state wants to pass a law to have legalized gambling?"

"Personally, I detest gambling. I'm so dead set against it — I'll bet 2 to 1 they'll never legalize it."

McCaskey was playing in a big poker game. Suddenly he jumped up from the table and shouted, "Hold on! This game is crooked. Somebody isn't playing with the cards I dealt him."

Once a week several New York dress manufacturers met for a friendly poker game. One night Birnbaum lost five thousand dollars and the shock was so great he had a heart attack and died right at the table. Of course they had to finish the game, but when it was over the men were faced with the problem of how to break the news to the deceased's wife. Finally Kreps volunteered to tell the widow.

At two in the morning he went to the apartment and knocked on the door. Mrs. Birnbaum opened the door and said, "All right, where is he?"

"Missus," said Kreps, "I'm really sorry to have to tell you this, but your husband just lost five thousand dollars playing poker."

"Five thousand dollars!" she cried. "That bum lost five thousand dollars playing poker? He should drop dead!"

"Don't worry, he did."

Gambling Giggles

Lenvil entered a book store and purchased two leatherbound Bibles.

"One of them," he explained, "is for myself. The other is for a guy at our shop I'm trying to convert. Lot of gambling going on and he's the ringleader."

As the clerk wrapped up the volumes, she remarked, "I hope you succeed in converting him."

"I do too," said Lenvil. "The other guys bet me five to three I couldn't."

"You want to make money in Las Vegas?"

"How?"

"Well, when you throw the dice — throw them as far away as possible."

"You lucky in cards?"

"Nah! Even when I'm cheating I can't win."

Renfield, a notorious poker addict, always in a jam with his wife over his all-night poker sessions, was faced with some real trouble on his way home from the office. He ran into Shanna, an old flame. Shanna still looked seductively attractive, so Renfield invited her to a nearby cocktail lounge for a drink. Time passed quickly and it was early morning when he walked into the house and faced his wife.

"Well," she snapped, "what's your alibi?"

Renfield decided to give it to her straight.

"Honey, it was just one of those things. I ran into an old girlfriend and we had a drink, and before we knew it, it was three in the morning. Well, I had to take her home, and —."

"Don't lie to me!" interrupted his wife. "How much did you lose playing poker tonight?"

**The only way to double your money
is to fold it over and put it back in your pocket.**

A psychiatrist informed Coslet, "You're cured. You are no longer a compulsive gambler. If you wish, you may call your wife and tell her the news. Use my phone or the one in the reception room."

Coslet thought for a moment, then he took a coin from his pocket, flipped it in the air, and said, "Heads or tails?"

Did you hear about the ex-GI who has a terrific business going?

He makes dice out of Ivory — for floating crap games.

Parfitt, a poker addict, went insane from gambling and was sent to a mental institution. For years they served the poor fellow toast for breakfast.

Parfitt always snapped up the toast, peeked at it as he held it close to his chest, and then said, "I pass." Then he pushed it aside.

Every day for 15 years he did the same thing. Then one morning they served him raisin toast. It had just one raisin in the middle of the slice.

Parfitt looked at the slice of toast and shouted, "I open."

Ricky was walking down the street dressed only in a barrel when a police officer stopped him.

"Are you a poker player?" asked the cop.

"Not me," replied Ricky, "but I just left a couple of guys who are!"

Sloan had a gambling problem all his life and finally went to a psychiatrist for a cure.

"Did the shrink help you?" asked a friend.

"Oh, yeah," said Sloan. "I used to go to the race track every day — now I only go when it's open."

Gambling Giggles

Fast Freddie was buying drinks for everybody after a highly successful poker game in the back room of Buzzy's Bar in Buffalo.

A friend said, "Without question, you are about the biggest gambler in town, Freddie. How come you never play the horses?"

Fast Freddie smiled from ear to ear and said, "Because I don't get to deal the horses."

Gilbert, an inveterate horse player, discovered some horrifying news. His daughter had contracted leukemia and she needed constant blood transfusions. The doctor informed him the cost could run up to $20,000.

Gilbert asked his brother-in-law to loan him the money.

"I can't do it!" said the brother-in-law. "If I give you $20,000 you'll go right out and bet it on the horses."

"No, I won't," said Gilbert. "I've got money for that."

Skeeter was talking to Toby, his friend down at the pool hall. "For three nights straight, I dream about salami, bologna and liverwurst. Is that a hunch, or ain't it? I go to the track and in one race three horses by the names of Salami, Bologna and Liverwurst are running. So I bet on all three to win —."

"Which horse won?" asked Toby.

"A long shot by the name of Cold Cuts."

Mrs. Newberry, a religious and charitable woman, went about doing things for the down and out. She noticed a homeless person standing on the same corner day after day. Determined to do something for him, she thrust an envelope into his hand. On it Mrs. Newberry had written "never despair" and in it she enclosed two dollars.

The next day she was surprised to see the man appear on her doorstep and drop a letter into her mailbox.

Mrs. Newberry opened it and read, "Never Despair won and paid 28 to 1. Enclosed find $56."

New Yorkers took the bookmaker off
the street so they could go into business
for themselves. It's called off-track betting.

CHILD SUPPORT

Paying off a gambling debt.

"There's a horse running in this race that's a sure thing.
He's had adrenalin shots in his hind legs, codeine in his
food and right now he's smoking marijuana!"
"Do you really think he'll win?"
"Don't know, but he'll be the happiest horse in the race!"

BANK PRESIDENT: Where's the cashier?
MANAGER: Gone to the races.
BANK PRESIIDENT: Gone to the races in business hours?
MANAGER: Yes, sir. It's his last chance
of making the books balance.

Miss Balderston brought a group of her fifth-grade boys
to the track to study the horses — how they eat, where they
sleep — all their habits. After a couple of hours they all had
to go to the boys room so she went along to help them. She
buttoned one, helped another. Went right down the line. As
she was zipping up the last one she said, "Say, are you in
the fifth?"
He said, "Heck no, ma'm, I'm riding Brown Beauty in
the sixth!"

**Gamblers are nice people. A Coral Gables guy
always observes "Be Kind to Animals Week" —
all the money he earns, he gives to the horses.**

Gambling Giggles

"I just want to know the truth. Is it really wrong to bet on the horses?"

"Yes, the way I do."

KENTUCKY DERBY CONVERSATION

WANDA:	Could you lend me a safety pin?
CLYDE:	Sorry, I don't have one.
ANNOUNCER:	
(*over loudspeaker*)	They're off!
She fainted.	

What's the secret method for returning from Las Vegas with a small fortune?

Go with a large fortune.

Some people don't give Texans enough credit for being good gamblers. Last month a big Dallas stockbroker went to Las Vegas in a $40,000 Cadillac and returned to Big "D" in a $100,000 bus.

Jana and Kip had been married twelve years. One morning at breakfast Jana looked perturbed. "You had a very restless night, dear," she said, "and what's more, you kept repeating a woman's name in your sleep. Who is Henrietta?"

"Oh - er," stammered Kip. "The fact is, honey, Henrietta is a horse I bet on yesterday. It won and paid eight to one and here is your share."

That evening when he returned from work, Jana returned to the attack. "About that horse, Henrietta, that you bet on yesterday."

"Yes," he grunted.

"Well," Jana screamed, "she called you up on the phone this afternoon."

Gedren, the jockey, had just booted home a long shot and was greeted excitedly by the horse's owner. "Tell me, please, what it was that you whispered in my horse's ear to make him run so fast."

"Oh," said Gedren, "all I did was recite poetry to him."

"Poetry?" screamed the owner in disbelief.

"Sure," answered the jockey.

"Roses are red,

"Violets are blue,

"Horses that lose

"Are made into glue."

Stoller, in a flashy plaid jacket, looked out of place in the clubhouse of the Kentucky race track. As one blue-blood watched, Stoller went up to the window and placed $60,000 to win on Royal Flush. A little later, Stoller went back to bet another $60,000. In a few minutes he stood up with an even bigger wad in his hand. The Kentucky horseman felt a pang of compassion and stopped the guy saying, "You're not going to bet on Royal Flush again, are you?"

"So what if I am?" announced Stoller in a thick New York accent.

"Royal Flush has absolutely no chance to win. He doesn't have any speed. I know, because I own him."

"Maybe so," said the New Yorker, "but it's gonna be a damn slow race. I own the other four horses."

SPORTING SPOOFS

**The difference between a college athlete
and a professional is that the pro is paid by check.**

"Harriet, is it true that your husband is a linguist?"
"Yes, Emmaline, he speaks three languages: golf,
football and baseball."

Mrs. Crane was a TV football widow and she had
reached the breaking point. Mr. Crane sat hunched before
his fifth televised game of the weekend.
"You lousy crumb!" she cried. "You love football more
than me!"
"That's true, baby," he retorted, "but I love you more
than basketball."

"What'sa matta, Tony? You look kinda down today."

"Aaah, my wife keeps buggin' me that I ignore the family during football season. That's ridiculous! During the commercials I make it a point to talk with my wife and two sons ... or is it three?"

Mrs. Agostino stood tearfully before the judge trying to get a divorce. "Your Honor, my husband isn't interested in me. All he talks about from morning till night is horses. He doesn't even remember our wedding day."

"That's a lie!" declared Agostino. "We got married the day Foolish Pleasure won the Kentucky Derby."

NEWS ITEM

A new organization has been formed called Athletics Anonymous. When you get the urge to play golf, baseball, or any other game involving physical activity, they send somebody over to drink with you until the urge passes.

Bert and Pinky, two basketball freaks, were sitting next to each other at Madison Square Garden.

"How'd you get such good seats for the playoffs?"

"Through my uncle. He's a sports mechanic."

"What's that?" asked Bert.

"He fixes ballgames," said Pinky.

"Snuffy's a real sports nut!"

"That's true, everybody knows it. He loves to bowl and he claims he's never lost a ball."

If you can't hear a pin drop, then there's something wrong with your bowling.

Bernie was a bowling fiend who played every Thursday evening. One Thursday he left the house and never came back. Apparently he vanished off the face of the earth.

Exactly five years later to the day, Bernie returned home, and his overjoyed wife started telephoning all their friends.

"What are you doing?" he asked.

"I'm going to throw a homecoming party for you!" replied his smiling wife.

"Oh, no you don't baby!" Bernie barked. "Not on my bowling night!"

At the amusement center, the woman in charge of the bowling concession noticed Marie, a pretty young secretary, bowling first with her right hand, and then with her left.

"Miss," she said, "you'll improve your average if you just concentrate on one hand."

"Oh," replied Marie, "I'm worried about my weight. I want to take some off this side and some off that side."

"I like bowling. I'd rather bowl than eat."

"Doesn't your wife object?"

"No, she'd rather play bridge than cook."

A little white-haired man bent over, picked up two bowling balls, and threw them down the alley for a strike. He picked up two more and repeated the incredible feat. Wally walked up to the geezer and asked him how he did it.

"When I was 18 years old," explained the old fellow, "I didn't feel too well so I told the foreman where I worked. He told me that if I wanted to feel good I'd have to drink a quart of whiskey every morning before breakfast, smoke three cartons of cigarettes a day, and go out with at least five women every night."

"What a fabulous life you've led," said Wally. "How old are you?"

"Twenty-four!" said the old man.

The traveling minister had finished his sermon in the prairie town and asked, "Now, how many of you would like to go to heaven?"

Everyone raised a hand except for a small boy sitting in the front row.

The minister looked down at the lad and asked, "Don't you want to go to heaven?"

"I'd like to," said the youngster, "but I got hockey practice at 2 o'clock."

Dwayne and Chantal were at a college basketball game. Dwayne was a real patriot about his school, and in the middle of the game he pointed down at the court. "See that big guy down there playing forward?" he asked the girl. "I think he's going to be our best man next year."

"Oh, darling," she cried, "this is so sudden!"

What's basketball?

It's a sport where 10 superb black athletes in perfect physical condition run up and down a court in front of 15,000 white spectators who could use the exercise.

Why are so many young basketball stars unable to get college scholarships?

They can jump, they can run, they can shoot, but they can't pass.

What do pro basketball players do when they're accused of taking drugs?

Hire a crack attorney.

How many college basketball players does it take to change a light bulb?

Only one, but he gets 37 credit hours for it.

Did you hear about the college basketball star who got his diploma in just three terms?

Carter's, Reagan's and Bush's.

The college assistant football coach was hired to recruit in the West Virginia hills. After a few days on the road, he showed up with a gigantic six-foot-eight flanker back who could run, block and catch passes like Jerry Rice. The head coach was really impressed, but he had doubts about the giant's formal education.

"He's OK," said the assistant coach.

"I'll give him a test," said the head coach. He turned to the huge kid and asked, "All right, can you tell me how much 9 and 9 is?"

The giant thought for a second, then said, "I believe that 9 and 9 is 15."

"See, Coach, I told you he wasn't dumb," said the assistant. "He missed by only three."

A Pittsburgh woman was reading a news item from the *Post Gazette* when she turned to her husband.

"Look, dear," she said, "there's a report here about a man who traded his wife for a season ticket to the Steelers' games. You wouldn't do anything like that, would you?"

"Of course not! Why the season is nearly half over!"

BASEBALL

Fifteen minutes of action
crammed into three hours.

Miss Buckner stood up before her class and asked, "Can anyone tell me where Houston is?"

She was shocked out of her shoes because Dirk, the dullest boy in the class raised his hand. Mrs. Buckner said, "All right, Dirk, you may answer."

"Houston is playing in New York," said the boy.

211

Randolph, the coach of a Little League baseball team, called over one of his players and said, "I want to explain some of the principles of sportsmanship to you."

The little boy said, "Yes, sir!"

"We don't believe in temper tantrums, screaming at the umpires, using bad language or sulking when we lose," railed Randolph. "Do you understand?"

The kid said, "Yes, sir!"

"All right then, do you think you can explain that to your father jumping around over there in the stands?"

Hawkins and Johnson were out hunting for the very first time. "Y'know," said Hawkins, "we been out here a whole day and haven't hit nothing yet."

"Yeah," said Johnson, "why don't we miss a couple of more times and then go home?"

The hunter was getting a bit frightened at the prospect of being totally lost. In frustration he screamed at his guide, "I thought you said you were the best guide in Maine."

"Yes, I truly am," replied the guide. "But I think we're in Vermont."

Lombardi, McTavish and Cusick, three amateur hunters, started out in Canada's big game country. They agreed before leaving camp that if they became separated, the call for help would be to shoot three times in the air.

Treking through the wilderness they soon were split up, and Cusick quickly became lost. Remembering the agreement, he shot three times into the air, but there was no answer. He shot three times again. Still no reply. It was getting dark, and once again Cusick shot three times into the air. And still, no one came to help him.

"Golly," mumbled Cusick to himself, "somebody better come along pretty soon. I'll be running out of arrows."

Sporting Spoofs

Rutledge and Horton had been in the woods for hours and there was no getting around the fact that they were lost.

"What're we gonna do?" asked Rutledge in panic. "We're lost!"

"Don't get excited," said Horton. "Shoot an extra deer. The game warden'll find us inside of thirty seconds."

BUTCHER: I'm sorry, but we have no ducks today. How about a nice leg of lamb?

HUNTER: Don't be silly. I can't tell my wife I shot a leg of lamb, can I?

Crost, Hanson and Weinberg, three duck hunters, had just beached their boat when they spotted the game warden bearing down on them. Weinberg leaped out of the boat and ran down the beach with the officer in hot pursuit. After a long chase, the hunter gave up and the warden demanded to see his license.

"What's the matter with you?" asked the angry officer. "Why'd you run from me. The duck season is open and you have the proper license."

"Well, you see," answered Weinberg, "the other guys didn't have."

"That's a magnificent stuffed bear," declared the visiting hunter. "Where did you bag him?"

"Northern Ontario, on a hunting trip with my father."

"What's he stuffed with?"

"My father."

Hewie never stopped bragging to anybody who would listen about his prowess as a crack shot.

On one bird-hunting trip, Hewie took careful aim and fired, but the bird flew on undisturbed in the blue sky. The marksman watched it in dazed silence for a moment, then dashed his gun to the ground and cried out, "Fly on, you gol-durned silly fool bird. Fly on with your gol-durned heart shot out!"

Randy got permission to go deer hunting with his dad in Wyoming and he was thrilled about it. Late one afternoon, he hurried back to camp and on the way he met their guide, Tony Poulos.

"Tony," he said to the guide, "are all the fellows out of the woods yet?"

"Yep," said Poulos.

"Dad and all the rest of them?"

"Yep. Your father and all the rest, " said the guide.

"You're sure?" asked Randy.

"Sure, I'm sure," said Tony.

"And they're all safe?"

"Every one of them," said the guide.

"Oh, boy!" said Randy. "Then I've shot a deer."

STYLES: I just met a great big bear
back there in the woods.

THORPE: Good! Did you give him
both barrels?

STYLES: The heck with both barrels.
I gave him the whole darned gun.

Clovis and Vestal were in the Tennessee northwoods enjoying some home brew in a cabin they'd rented for the weekend. Each boasted of his hunting prowess, and soon the bragging got out of hand.

"I'll betcha $50 I can go out into the woods right now and be back with a bearskin within the hour," Clovis finally flat out threatened.

Vestal was just drunk enough to let him try it.

But the hour came and went. No Clovis. Two hours went buy. Still no Clovis. Three hours later there came a knock at the door. Vestal opened it and there in the doorway stood a huge brown bear.

"Your name Vestal Doyce?" asked the bear.

"Y-y-yes," stammered Vestal.

"You know a guy named Clovis Thetchel?"

"Yes, I do," replied Vestal.

"Well, he owes you 50 bucks."

Sporting Spoofs

Caldwell was telling Larker and Drake about his trip into the wilds. "I got into the middle of the field and met the biggest bear I ever saw in my life," said Caldwell. "He was at least 12 feel tall and his paws were a full 12 inches wide.

"There was only one tree in that whole field, and I ran for it with everything I had. That tree was old and tall, and the first branch was 30 feet from the ground."

"Good Lord!" cried Larker. "Whadya do?"

"Well, the bear was right behind me breathing down my neck. So I jumped up for that branch."

"Did you make it?" asked Drake.

"No, not going up. But I caught it coming down!"

Did you hear about the guy planning to manufacture glass-bottom boats so the fish can see how big the guy is they got away from?

Willard was the best known hunter back in the West Virginia hills. One day the boys were sitting on the porch of the general store and an old hillbilly asked Willard to tell them his most hair-raising experience.

"It was deep in the woods back when I was younger," he began slowly. "I was ploddin' along mindin' my own business when suddenly a huge grizzly sneaked up behind me. He pinned my arms to my sides and started to squeeze the breath out of me. My gun fell out of my hands. The bear stooped down, picked up the gun and was pressin' it into my back."

"What'd yew do?" everybody asked.

"What in the world could I do?" sighed Willard. "I married his daughter."

A mental patient from the state asylum was fishing. Actually, he had the rod and reel — but his empty hook was dangling in a small glass fishbowl. A visitor walked up and tried to humor him. "How many have you caught so far?"

The lunatic laughed. "You're the fifth!"

Simmons left Manhattan in a a brand new, color-coordinated fishing costume and headed for an out-of-the way lake in Maine. A barefoot kid watched his ludicrous antics for some time and finally hazarded a, "How many fish you caught, mister?"

"None yet," said the New Yorker.

"That's not bad," said the kid. "Feller dressed even funnier'n you fished here for two weeks and didn't get any more than you got in half an hour!"

One night at the fisherman's club, Morrow was describing his toughest catch. "After three hours I landed this terrific monster of the sea," he said.

"I saw the pictures and he was only six inches long," said one member.

"Sure," admitted Morrow, "but in three hours of fighting, a fish can lose a lot of weight."

There was a young fellow named Fisher
Who was fishing for a fish in a fissure;
    Then a cod with a grin
    Pulled the fisherman in,
Now they're fishing the fissure for Fisher.

The Sunday school teacher frowned at little Rudy when he came in late one Sunday morning. "Why weren't you on time?" she asked.

"I wanted to go fishing this morning," Rudy said, "but my father wouldn't let me."

"You're a very lucky boy to have a father like that," said the teacher. "And did your father make it clear to you why you shouldn't go fishing?"

"Sure," said Rudy. "He told me there wasn't enough bait for both of us."

Sporting Spoofs

One day Harold was sitting on the banks of a stream, waiting for the fish, when a stranger came along.

"Catch any yet?" the stranger asked.

"Nope."

"That's funny," said the stranger. "I heard this was a fine place for trout."

"It must be," said Harold. "They refuse to leave it."

Turk could not face another weekend without fishing. Saturday morning he drove eight miles down a California back road to a place marked *Private* and went through a gate that said, *Keep Out — Trespassers Will Be Prosecuted.* Then he walked to a lake where there was a sign planted, *No Fishing Allowed.* The fishing season hadn't opened and Turk didn't have a license, but he was having himself a wonderful time.

Finally a stranger walked up.

"Any luck?" asked the stranger.

"Couldn't be better. This is a great spot. Got me over a hundred pounds of the biggest trout you ever saw in the back of my car."

"Is that so? By the way," said the stranger, "do you know who I am?"

"Nope."

"Well, I'm the game warden," said the stranger.

"Oh, my goodness!" gulped the fisherman. "Do you know who I am?"

"Nope."

"Well, meet the biggest damn liar in the United States."

Finch was telling his buddy Waldron about a fish he nearly caught in the Bahamas. His description of the event was beyond any degree of reality.

"About the size of a whale, wasn't it?" Waldron said with a big smile.

"A whale!" echoed Finch. "Listen, pal, I was baitin' with whales!"

217

An atomic scientist went on a vacation. In his absence a sign was hung on his office door reading, *Gone Fission!*

GAME WARDEN: Don't you know that fishing here is prohibited?

PAPADAPOULOS: Fishing? I'm only trying to teach this poor little worm to swim.

Parish and Carlton were sitting on a bridge with their lines dangling in the water.

"I'll bet you 20 bucks that I catch a fish before you do," said Parish.

"You're on," replied Carlton.

Pretty soon Parish got a nibble on his line and became so excited he fell into the river.

"Hold it!" cried Carlton. "If you're going to dive for them, the bet is off."

If a fisherman goes home and lies about the size of "the one that got away," do you think a fish goes home and lies about the size of the bait he stole?

McDougal was fishing the Klamath River in Oregon when he was caught and arrested for catching 32 trout — 20 more than the law allows.

"How do you plead?" asked the judge.

"Guilty," replied the fisherman.

"Fifty dollars and costs," decreed the judge.

"I'm glad to pay it, your honor," said McDougal, "and could I have several copies of the court record, as well, to show my friends?"

"How'd you do on your vacation?"
"I caught a fish that was so big it took two men to carry the photograph."

When is the only time a fisherman tells the truth?
When he calls another fisherman a liar.

Daily and Lang were taking a fisherman's holiday. As they sat in an old rowboat, their poles poking out into the salt air, the lines dangling lifelessly in the water, neither man moved a muscle. Then suddenly, after three hours of this, Lang got restless.
"Dammit," complained Daily, "that's the third time you shuffled your feet in an hour. Did you come here to fish or to dance?"

There are two kinds of fishermen: those who fish for sport and those who catch something.

TENNIS

The only game in which
love means nothing.

Did you hear about the University of Southern California coed who was so cockeyed she could watch a tennis match without moving her head?

A suntanned young giant arrived late at a tennis tournament and sat down. "Whose game?" he asked.
Marion, a pretty steno next to him, looked up and said, "I am."

When was the first tennis game played in biblical times?
When Moses served in Pharoah's court.

"Why's your arm in a sling?"
"I've got a real bad case of tennis elbow. I was playing doubles with my wife and when I didn't return an easy lob she got mad and hit me on the arm with her racket."

Lisa left Los Angeles to visit some staid and conservative relatives in Boston. After a few days she commented on the restraint and reserve of the people she was meeting.

"Remember," said her aunt, "this is Boston. Here it's the family that counts. We are interested in breeding."

"Well, in California we think breeding is fun, too," said Lisa. "But we also manage a little tennis now and then."

ALICE: I love tennis. I could play this game forever.
BYRON: Gosh, don't you ever want to improve?

Harold had been jogging in the park one morning and noticed a couple engaged in a heated tennis match. He stopped to watch for a few moments. As he started to leave on his run, he spotted two tennis balls at his feet. He picked them up and stuck them in his sweat pants.

Harold continued on his jog and soon was joined by a very pretty blonde. They chatted casually, but she kept staring at the two huge bulges in his pants. Finally, Harold caught her eye and said, "Oh, those are tennis balls."

"Oh, my," exclaimed the girl, "that must really hurt. I've got tennis elbow and I know how that feels!"

**Tennis is not a matter of life
or death — it's more important than that.**

Myrtle and Phoebe met at the supermarket. "How is your husband getting along with his golf?" asked Myrtle.

"Much better," said Phoebe. "The children are now allowed to watch him."

Kopel was a par golfer, Buzzi a rank duffer. To even up things, Kopel gave his friend a stroke a hole. Buzzi began playing over his head and, with his one-stroke advantage, was able to tie or beat his partner on quite a few holes.

The ninth hole proved to be a short one — 168 yards. Kopel stepped up, swung his club, and hit a beauty. The ball hit the green, bounced twice, and rolled into the cup. A hole in one!

"Boy," Kopel chortled, "just try to beat that!"

Buzzi stood there a moment, then suddenly his face lit up. "I win this hole!" he announced.

"Are you crazy?"

"It's my hole," he repeated.

"How come?"

"I claim my stroke!"

BULLETIN BOARD NOTICE IN A PRO SHOP

If You Drink, Don't Drive.
Use a Three Wood.

The heaviest storm of the year piled snow in deep drifts, forcing homeowners to dig their way out. Vitale peeked through the window to watch his neighbor, Mason, struggling all morning with the heavy labor.

Finally Vitale ventured outside and said to Mason, "By golly, you've been workin' all morning without even taking a break!"

"When I feel myself faltering," answered Mason, "I'm heartened by my wife's words, 'Keep shoveling or I'll smash your clubs!'"

"How're you hittin' 'em?"

"I'm playing so bad I'm just gonna buy a bucket of balls and practice my drop!"

Derrick had been playing good golf despite having a caddie who had the hiccups. Derrick was on the last hole of the round and about to win the match when he overshot the hole. Angrily, he snapped, "Look at what your damned hiccups have done! They've ruined my game."

"But I didn't hiccup on that one," objected the caddie.

"I know," snarled the golfer, "but I allowed for it."

TEACHER: What becomes of boys who use bad language when they play marbles?
RAYMOND: I guess they grow up and play golf.

Elmer hit a long ball on a Houston course fairway and his partner Cyril remarked, "Um, um! That's a plumanelly."

"What's a plumanelly?"

"Plum outta sight, an' ne'lly on the green."

Merle and Charleen were immediately attracted to each other and, after a whirlwind courtship, began to discuss marriage. "We are mature people," he said to her, "and I want you to know, now, that I'm a golfaholic. I play most afternoons and every weekend year 'round."

"Thanks, Merle, for your honesty," she replied. "I'll be honest with you. I'm a hooker."

"Oh, don't worry about that," he answered. "Just concentrate on keeping your backswing smooth and your wrists straight."

Sporting Spoofs

Phil and Carey teed off on the fourteenth hole of a woodsy Oregon course. As they drove down the center of the fairway they discovered a man rolling on the ground, laughing convulsively.

Phil then heard a voice shouting obscenities over in the rough, and he spotted a golfer beating the tall grass unmercifully. "Hey," said Phil to the golfer on the ground, "why don't you go over and help your partner find his ball?"

"Because he didn't lose his ball," chortled the man. "He lost his club!"

Did you hear about the guy who was addicted to golf and married a woman whose passion was auctions and they both talked in their sleep?

He'd say "Fore," and she'd say, "Four and a half."

"At the fourth hole I left a poop."
"That can happen to anyone."
"Yes, but I followed through."

"This new ball I got is fantastic."
"What's so great about it?"
"It's got a sonic beep. You hit it into the rough, you find it immediately."
"What happens if it goes into the water?"
"You kidding? The minute it hits the water it releases a little red, white and blue flag that floats to the top — you can find it immediately."
"That really is fantastic. Where'd you get it?"
"I found it."

**Golf is like business — you drive hard
to get to the green and then wind up in a hole.**

McCreedy and Phillips were having a brew at a Boston beer hall.

"How come I don't see you out on the municipal course lately?" asked McCreedy.

"I've had real bad luck with golf," replied Phillips. "My minister suggested that before every swing, I bow my head, close my eyes, and pray. So I bowed my head, closed my eyes, and prayed — and somebody stole my clubs."

Osborne loved golf but it was becoming increasingly difficult for him to play. He complained to the club president. "I'm nearsighted. I lose balls. I can't play with glasses, they keep falling off."

"Why don't you team up with Cromwell?" suggested the head of the club.

"The old man?" exclaimed Osborne. "He must be 95 years old and he gets around in a wheelchair."

"You're right. He is up in age. But the old guy is farsighted. You hit the ball and he'll be able see it and tell you where it went. Try it! What have you got to lose?"

The next day Osborne and the old man sitting in his wheelchair were up on the first tee. Osborne took a tremendous swing and the ball sailed more than two hundred yards up the fairway. "Boy, that felt good," shouted Osborne. "Where did it go?"

"I can't remember!" said Cromwell.

MONEY MIRTH

**There are lots of things more important
than money, but you need money to buy them.**

Mead was being interviewed for employment. "What about your last job?" asked the personnel director.

"I cleaned out the bank," replied the young man.

"Janitor or president?"

Mrs. Garabaldi phoned the bank in a terrible huff. "My check has been returned marked 'Lack of Funds,'" she complained angrily.

"That's correct," said the bank manager.

"Impossible!" snapped the woman. "I made a substantial deposit just last week!"

"True," replied the banker. "Unfortunately your deposit wasn't large enough to cover our payroll."

**It's true that money can't buy
love, but it makes shopping more fun.**

225

The savings and loan scandals affected all Americans but the thrift industry in California was particularly rife with rotten apples. In Sacramento, a flamboyant bank mogul was tried for fraud and embezzlement.

"This man was caught red handed," the prosecutor charged. "We have a video tape of him leaving the bank with a suitcase full of cash!"

"I'm not a thief," argued the banker. "I was taking that money home to show my family what kind of work I do."

Did you hear about the latest S&L that went under? They had more vice presidents than depositors.

A Mexican bank recently contacted a Dallas S&L: "We understand that Harold Fritz was a tried and trusted employee of yours," they wrote.

The Dallas S&L answered: "Mr. Fritz was trusted, and he'll be tried if he ever sets foot here again."

A bank president was in conference with a store owner whose loan payments were delinquent.

"Business is terrible," complained the merchant.

"Well, the President says that business is great," argued the banker.

"Yeah," nodded the shopkeeper sadly, "but he's got a better location."

Two troubled S&L officers were having cocktails at the Top of the Mark in San Francisco.

"You look down, pal," said one. "Why the long face?"

"A few weeks ago I had everything," replied his colleague. "Plenty of cash, a beach house, a sports car and the love of a gorgeous woman. Then bang, one morning my wife walks in!"

Money Mirth

Before the scandals broke, a lot of California S&L officers were spending lavishly on big parties, expensive boats and opulent houses. The head of a Los Angeles thrift threw a big bash aboard his yacht.

"I wish I had the money for a boat like this," observed one partygoer.

"Yeah," said the banker, "so do I."

Some Texas bank executives also did their share of living high on the hog. Big ticket luxury items were flying out of the shops. The only thing faster than the speed of light was a yuppie S&L officer in a Porsche on his way to a Rolex sale.

BANKER

Someone who lends you
an umbrella when the
sun shines and wants it
back when it rains.

After just a few weeks, a small restaurant went bankrupt. The owner placed this sign in the window:
Returned to Lender — Opened by Mistake.

Responding to all the bad press, banks are trying to win back depositors by expanding their hours. In North Dakota, the widow Faskens decided it was safe to reopen her savings account. She called a bank at 6 a.m. and the president picked up the phone.

"What time do you open for deposits?" she asked.

"What time can you get here?" he replied.

**The only trouble with money
is you can't use it more than once.**

227

A yuppie S&L officer was speeding along Highway 1 in his new Mercedes when he missed a curve, flew over a cliff and totalled his car. A passing motorist found him mangled and bleeding.

"My Mercedes!" sobbed the banker. "My beautiful new car ... my CD player ... my cellular phone! Gone! All of them gone!"

"Good grief, man!" said the motorist. "How can you cry over a silly car when your left arm has been severed above the elbow!"

The banker looked down. "My Rolex!" he wailed, "my beautiful gold Rolex!"

A BANK IS A PLACE:

— that has a drive-up window so the real owners of your car can see it now and then.
— that will gladly lend money to those who prove they don't really need any.
— that takes deposits from the poor so it can lend to the rich.
— that makes a profit giving out credit cards so people will buy things they can't afford with money they never had.

Did you hear the latest thing Colorado banks are giving customers who have everything?

A calendar to remind them when the payments are due.

Elmer Winkle died. At his funeral, his old friend George was surprised to see six bankers acting as pallbearers. After the service, George approached the funeral director.

"I don't understand," he said. "Elmer hated bankers. Why were they his pall bearers?"

"Mr. Winkle put it in his will," replied the mortician. "He said they carried him so long while he was alive, they might as well finish the job."

Money Mirth

Blauser read the complicated instructions for the automatic teller machine, but remained confused. He walked over to one of the bank officers.

"Excuse me," he said, "but I was wondering if you could possibly help me out."

"Why certainly," said the officer, smiling. "Go right through that door over there."

Standing in line at the bank, one business person said to another, "What really infuriates me about banking is that you give them your money freely, but when you try to borrow any they want to know if you're good for it!"

The bank teller had just been robbed for the third time by the same man. The detective asked, "Did you notice anything specific about the criminal?"

"Actually, yes," said the teller, "he seems to dress better each time."

Hutchinson stopped by his bank to cash a check. Just as he entered the lobby, a man holding a large bag came running past him, headed for the exit. Suddenly, the security guard came dashing out, followed by several bank employees.

The guard tackled the man with the bag, handcuffed him and hauled him back into the bank.

Hutchinson was shaking like a leaf. As he approached the teller's window, he couldn't resist finding out more about what he had just seen. In a trembling voice he asked, "Was that really a robbery?"

"Oh, no sir," replied the teller. "That was only our substantial penalty for early withdrawal."

Money doesn't talk anymore
— it just goes without saying.

When it comes to money leave us not forget the financial analysts, investment counselors, and CPA's (which does not stand for Cleaning, Pressing and Alterations).

CPA

An accountant who shows you how
to save almost enough money to pay his bill.

There's good news and bad news about members of the financial community.

The good news is that a busload of CPA's went over a cliff.

The bad news is that there were three empty seats.

Did you hear about the CPA who has an office over a big Boston bank?

He proudly brags that his assets are over sixty-five million dollars.

What is an auditor? Someone who comes in immediately after the battle is fought.

Some auditors are accompanied by lawyers who then strip the bodies.

"Is your company big enough to have a bookkeeper?"
"Oh, yes, we have a bookkeeper who's shy and retiring. He's shy $20,000. That's why he's retiring."

**Money can't buy you love, but
it puts you in a great bargaining position!**

Money Mirth

A CPA lady from Rye,
Had a shape like a capital I;
    When they said, "It's too bad,"
    She learned how to pad,
Which shows you that figures can lie.

Rothman was trying desperately for a bookkeeper's job in a Manhattan firm. He was asked by his prospective employer, "Can you do double entry?"

"Yes, sir. In fact I can do triple entry!" replied the out-of-work bookkeeper.

"*Triple* entry?" asked the owner.

"Sure," replied Rothman. "One entry for the working partner showing the true profits. Another entry for the silent partner showing a very small profit. And a third for the Internal Revenue showing a big loss!"

"You can always tell a guy's profession by observing his introduction to a pretty woman."

"How's that?"

"The lawyers may kiss her hand. The sales people may ask her out. But the accountants — they wire the home office for instructions."

A Southern Pacific express train sped along the edge of one of the biggest cattle ranches in Texas. Wallach gazed intently at the huge herds grazing on the thick grass. When the boundary line of the ranch was finally reached, he turned to Stanbury occupying the seat with him and said, "Quite a herd of cattle on that ranch. I counted 12,476 head."

"That's incredible," said Stanbury. "I happen to be the owner of that ranch and I know that I own exactly 12,476 head of cattle. How on earth did you manage to count them from a train that was going 60 miles an hour?"

"Oh, it's easy if you know the system," said the accountant. "I just count their legs and divide by four."

Cornwaite complained to his friend Sloan that he had been ordered to give up wine, women, and song.

"Why don't you see another doctor?" advised Sloan.

"But it wasn't my doctor," cried Cornwaite. "It was my tax accountant."

ACCOUNTANT

One who checks up on the bookkeeper
to see if there are any accounts deceivable.

Melandry called all his creditors together to tell them he was going into bankruptcy.

"I'm into you guys for over five hundred thousand dollars," he told them. "Unfortunately, I can't pay a penny of what I owe anybody. If you want, you can cut me up in little pieces and divide my body among you."

"I vote we do it," shouted one of the creditors. "I'd like to have his gall."

Tax accountant to client: "I've got terrible news for you. Last year was the best year you ever had."

At a midwest college, the latest course was posted on the bulletin board at the beginning of the semester:

"Course in Accounting for Women."

After the sign had been up for a couple of days, someone went and put another sign under it:

"There is no accounting for women."

Money may talk, but today's dollar
doesn't have cents enough to say very much.

Money Mirth

Easterly and Strobe were up in a hot air balloon and realized they had gotten lost. They spotted a man on the ground and Easterly yelled down to him, "Where are we?"

The man replied, "You're in a hot air balloon."

Easterly looked over at his partner and said, "This guy's a CPA."

"How do you know?" asked Strobe.

"That's easy," said Easterly, "his information is totally correct and totally worthless."

What is the biggest fear in economics? Taking your little boy to a beginning math class and recognizing the person sitting next to him as your tax accountant.

Did you hear about the Philadelphia firm's accounting department that has a little red box on the wall with a sign saying: *In Case of Emergency Break Glass.*

Inside are two tickets to Peru.

BOOKKEEPER

A person who feels good
when things start looking black again.

Homel and Slaten were having lunch. "If you want to make a small fortune, look up my accountant," said Homel.

"He's that good?" asked Slaten.

"No," said Homel, "but there's a cash reward for his arrest and conviction."

Accountants are kidded unmercifully about not having a sense of humor. Thank goodness they don't understand most of the jokes.

Johnson showed up at the Nashville Internal Revenue office to discuss his tax return. Another man behind the desk said, "What is your name?"

"Andrew Jefferson Johnson!"

"That's impossible," retorted the government man. "My name is Andrew Jefferson Johnson. How do you spell it?"

The taxpayer picked up a pencil and wrote "X X X."

"That's the same way Ah spell mine," announced the tax collector. "But after that Ah put ..." He added, "X X X."

"What does that mean?"

"C.P.A."

FIRST PARTNER:	I don't like the new bookkeeper you hired. She limps and stutters.
SECOND PARTNER:	What of it?
FIRST PARTNER:	Why did you hire her?
SECOND PARTNER:	So she'll be easy to identify if she steals.

Insurance is a lot like wearing a hospital gown.
You're never covered as much as you think you are.

"My car is totaled. What shall I do?"

"What does your policy say?"

"I don't know. The words are too big to understand and the type is too small to read."

At Virginia Beach, a small boy was pestering his mother.

"Why can't I go swimming?" he whined.

"Because it's too dangerous," his mother replied.

"But Daddy is swimming."

"Yes, darling, but Daddy is insured."

Money Mirth

Bailey applied for life insurance and was put through a rigorous physical exam and then made to fill out an exhaustive questionnaire. Finally he sat before the examiner.

"And you swear under severe penalty of law that you do not indulge in any activity that might possibly compromise your health?" the examiner demanded.

"Well," gulped Bailey, "I ... uh ... sometimes breathe during smog alerts."

INSURANCE AGENT: How badly were you hurt in the accident?

CLAIMANT: I don't know until after I speak with my lawyer.

The insurance salesman tried every conceivable close but the prospect was just not buying. Finally, in desperation, the salesman said, "Okay, I've met my match. But as a favor, will you please sign this testimonial letter for me?"

The prospect read the letter:

This is to confirm that I will not buy any life insurance from you no matter how hard you work to convince me that I should.

"What kind of testimonial letter is this?" asked the prospect. "Who could you show this to without looking like a complete fool?"

"I'll show it to your wife," said the salesman, "right after you die."

"Why in the world would you write a policy on a man 98 years old?" the insurance inspector demanded.

"Well," explained the young agent, "I checked statistics and very few people at that age die each year."

235

A reluctant prospect was questioning the insurance agent. "How do I know your company will pay up promptly should I have a claim?"

"You wanna talk prompt!" the agent boasted. "Our company is on the tenth floor. A client of ours recently fell out of a 19th floor window of the same building and we handed him his check on the way down."

Southern Mutual Life wrote out a policy on Forbus Hardy. Mr. Hardy's premiums were paid on time for many years then suddenly they stopped. After several delinquent notices, the insurance company received this memo:
"Dear Sirs:
Sorry, unable to keep up with the premiums on Forbus Hardy. He died last May.
Yours truly, Mrs F. Hardy."

Daybright went into an insurance office to have his life insured. The agent said, "Do you ride a bicycle?"
"No!" answered Daybright.
"Drive a car?"
"No!"
"Motorcycle?"
"Heavens no!" said Daybright. "Nothing dangerous."
"Sorry sir, but we no longer insure pedestrians."

Perry, a Miami stockbroker, got a phone in his car. He couldn't wait to call his friend, Mitchell. "I'm calling you from my car," he told him.

Mitchell was enraged with envy. So he too bought a phone for his car and immediately called the stockbroker. "Perry," he said, "I'm calling you from my car."

"Excuse me Mitchell, my other phone is ringing."

You've got to give the average American family a lot of credit — they can't get along without it.

Money Mirth

Several Madison Avenue yuppie advertising execs were sipping Sonoma County chardonnay at an East Side bar and discussing their troubles.

Hard luck Sibley topped them all when he dejectedly explained, "I've got a wife, a secretary and a note from the bank — all overdue."

INFLATION

An economic misfortune
that can be offset by three things:
An investment counselor, an
investment plan and an oil well.

A Los Angeles financial planner was run over by a car and the police officer said to him, "Did you see the license number of the vehicle that hit you?"

"No I didn't," said the victim, "but I'd recognize his laugh anywhere."

"Would you like to see our model home?" asked the real estate broker.

"I sure would!" the prospective customer eagerly responded. "What time does she quit work?"

REAL ESTATE AGENT: Now, ma'am here's a house
                        without a flaw.
SOUTHERN BELLE: What do y'all walk on?

During the midwest drought people were afraid of buying a home with a dry well. They coined the warning: "Never trust a Realtor who wears a canteen."

A Hawaiian real estate salesman was showing Henderson some property near Honolulu and was pulling out all the stops. He finished up with, "Why, the climate's the best in the world. Do you know, no one ever dies here?"

Just then, a funeral procession came into view and wound slowly down the street. The agent removed his hat and said, "Poor old undertaker. Starved to death."

REALTOR

An expert at making
a mountain out of a molehill.

A builder was showing a new house to a prospect. The buyer stood in one room and the builder in the next. "Can you hear me?" asked the builder in a whisper.

"Just barely," replied the prospect.

"Can you see me?"

"Only faintly."

"Now them's walls for you, ain't they!" declared the builder with pride.

Did you hear about the guy whose condo was so small he was forced to buy condensed milk?

Still, he had no room for complaint.

Osgood bought a house near a river bank, despite the fact that the cellar seemed rather damp.

"Snug as a bug in a rug," assured the salesman. "This cellar is dryer than the Sahara Desert."

A month later Osgood charged into the real estate office prepared to wring the salesman's neck. "You and your Sahara Desert," he cried. "I put two mousetraps in that cellar, and when I went down to look at them this morning they had caught a flounder and a haddock!"

Money Mirth

"This house," said the real estate salesman, "has both its good points and its bad points. To show you I'm honest, I'm going to tell you about both. The disadvantages are that there is a big chemical plant one block south and a large slaughterhouse one block north. There's a glue factory on the east and a rubber factory a few blocks west of here!"

"What are the advantages?" inquired the prospect.

"The advantage is that the price is low and you can always tell which way the wind is blowing."

CALIFORNIA REAL ESTATE ADS

How would you like
to pay $500,000 for a
$100,000 house?
Wait until next year.

When the ad says:
"A great house as a whole"
What it really means is:
As a hole it's OK, but as
a house it's the pits.

When the ad says:
"Breathtaking sunken
living room"
What it really means is:
Hold your breath — this
baby's still sinking.

When the ad says:
"This house is totally waterproof"
What is really means is:
After a rain, not a drop will leak
out of the cellar.

The anxious Realtor was showing a house to a newly married couple. "This is the hobby room," the agent explained. "Do you folks have a hobby?"
"Oh, yes," said the young husband.
"And what is it?"
"Looking at new model homes."

INDIAN REAL ESTATE BROKERS

Escrows

Costs are to a Realtor what in-laws are to a marriage. You know you'll always have them, but you try to get rid of as many of them as you can.

Two Miami Beach matrons were chatting over lunch. "My husband is so good to me," said Sadie. "Last week he bought me a condominium."
"All well and good," said Gladys, "but if I was you I would still take the pill."

The Lenharts decided to move out to the suburbs. She had lots of free time to look for a new house, so she signed up with a real estate agent.
Mrs. Lenhart spent several weeks looking at houses but found something wrong with each one. She never liked one house well enough to have her husband look at it with her.
Finally, the salesman grew impatient. "Madam, why do you need a home?" he exploded. "You were born in a hospital, educated in a school, courted in an automobile, and married in a church. You live at hamburger stands and eat out of freezers and cans. You spend your mornings at the golf course, your afternoons at the bridge table, and your evenings at the movies. All you really need is a garage!"

Money Mirth

Anderson, a big Chicago wheeler-dealer developer owned a loft building, a marble quarry, a factory site, and a summer estate. He proposed to swap all this with Bilby who owned three condominiums, a small subdivision, a mini shopping mall, and a farm.

"He assumes an $80,000 mortgage on the loft building," explained Anderson to his wife, "and I take over a second mortgage on the subdivision. Get me?"

"I guess so," responded the wife, "but if you've got all the details so cleverly worked out, what the heck's holding up the deal?"

"I sign nothing," he declared, "till he gives me ten dollars in cash!"

"We just moved into our dream house."
"That's great."
"Yeah. It cost twice as much as we dreamed it would."

Sokol went to see Raney, the Realtor about renting a small store in a run-down neighborhood.

"I want $800 a month," said Raney.

This infuriated Sokol, but he thought he would show Raney up for a cheapskate. "I'll be more generous than you," he said. "I'll give you $825."

"I'm generous, too. You can have it for $775."

"No. I'll give you $850."

"No, $750."

"No!" shouted Sokol, "$875!"

"No!" shrieked Raney. "We're old friends! I'll give it to you for nothing as long as I live."

"Make it for as long as *I* live," said Sokol, "because I'm gonna take your proposition and when I do you're gonna drop dead."

**Never put off until tomorrow
what you can buy today — there
will probably be a higher tax on it tomorrow.**

Schneider applied to a finance agency for a job, but he had no experience. He was so intense the manager gave him a tough account with the promise that if he collected it, he would give him a job.

"This guy'll never collect it," he told his secretary. "It's that Temkin, the building contractor who's owed us that money for two years."

Two hours later, Schneider came back with the entire sum. "Amazing!" said the manager. "How did you do it?"

"Easy," replied Schneider. "I told him if he didn't pay up, I'd tell all his other creditors he paid us."

EMBARASSING MOMENT

Showing off your new Cadillac all over
town and then crashing into a Volkswagen
driven by your Internal Revenue Service agent.

An even more embarrassing moment belongs to a Pittsburgh stockbroker who was rummaging through the attic when he came across his wife's love letters — and they were dated last week.

Walt and Emmitt were on a coffee break in the computer company cafeteria. "There have been a lot of brilliant guys in the history of the world," said Walt. "Einstein was smart, and Sigmund Freud was pretty good. Henry Ford wasn't bad either. But the smartest guy I know is Wendell Cronin over in purchasing."

"What makes him so brilliant?" asked Emmitt.

"He got his salary raised six months ago, and his wife hasn't found out about it yet," explained Walt.

**With today's inflation,
there's no money in money!**

Money Mirth

A school teacher was cashing a check. The teller handed over used, worn bills.

"I hope you're not paranoid about micro-organisms," the teller apologized.

"Don't worry," said the teacher. "Micro-organisms couldn't live on my salary."

Pearce, an encyclopedia salesman, was driving on a back dirt road and got bogged down in a section that was deep mud. Just then a farmer came by and offered to pull him out with his tractor for 20 bucks.

After he was back on dry ground Pearce said to the farmer, "At those prices, I should think you'd be pulling people out of the mud night and day."

"Can't," said the farmer. "At night I haul water over to the road to make it muddy!"

Hoyt asked his accountant for a dependable rule-of-thumb for estimating the cost of living.

The accountant said, "Take your income, whatever it is, and add 25 percent."

Silow, a San Diego stockbroker, was working at his desk, when his secretary Marti burst in. The poor woman was absolutely frantic.

"Sir, th-there's an IRS agent outside. He's got an SEC official with him and another man who says he's a federal marshall. They have a subpoena for you. W-what should I tell them?"

"Marti, you're a nice person and a fine secretary," said the broker, "and I appreciate what you're doing, but my hiccups are already gone. Thank you."

**The nicest thing about money is that
it never clashes with anything you're wearing!**

The President of the United States called an influential broker on Wall Street to tell him personally, "The economy is in good shape again. The outlook is fantastic. In fact, if I weren't the President of the United States I'd be investing in the stock market."

The man replied, "Believe me, sir, if you weren't President of the United States, everyone would be investing in the stock market."

Chalmers inherited seven million dollars, but the will provided he had to accept it either in Chile or Brazil. He chose Brazil. In Brazil he had to choose between receiving his inheritance in coffee or nuts, he chose nuts. But then, suddenly, the bottom fell out of the nut market, while coffee went up $2 a pound. Chalmers lost everything.

He sold his watch for money to fly back to the United States. He had enough cash for a ticket to either Miami or New York. Chalmers chose Miami. Just before he took off, the New York plane came out on the runway — it was a brand new superjet. The Miami plane was a 1948 trimotor with a sway back and took half a day to get off the ground. It was filled with crying children and tethered goats. Then over the Andes one engine fell off. Chalmers crawled up to the cockpit and said, "Let me out if you want to save your lives. Give me a parachute."

"Okay," said the pilot, "but on this airline, anybody who bails out must wear two chutes."

Chalmers jumped from the plane and as he fell he tried to make up his mind which rip cord to pull. Finally, he chose the one on the left. It was rusty and the wire broke. He pulled the other handle. The chute opened, but its shroud lines snapped. In desperation Chalmers cried out, "St. Francis save me! Please! St. Francis save me!"

Suddenly a great hand reached down from Heaven, seized the poor man's wrist and let him dangle in midair. Then a gentle voice asked, "St. Francis Xavier or St. Francis of Assisi?"

HUMOR BIBLIOGRAPHY

There are very few judges
of humor and they don't agree.
— JOSH BILLINGS

To satisfy an insatiable comedy curiosity, the library
in my office includes countless volumes of jokes, gags,
quips, stories, poems, riddles and limericks. The following
list has been compiled especially for those who love humor
as well as those who earn their livelihood from it. There are
also titles on writing comedy and using humor as a power
for healing.

The San Francisco Public Library houses the most
complete collection of books on comedy in the United
States, possibly the world. It includes more than 17,000
volumes of wit and humor by the greatest humorists who
ever lived.

Attorney Nat Schmulowitz, a respected member of the
California legal profession and gifted storyteller, founded the
collection in 1947.

An entire wing has been set aside to store what has
become known to humor historians and lovers of comedy as
the **Schmulowitz Collection of Wit And Humor.**

Adams, Joey. From Gags to Riches. New York: Frederick Fell, Inc., 1946.

Adams, Joey. Joey Adams Joke Book. New York: Frederick Fell, Inc., 1952.

Adams, Joey. Joey Adams Joke Dictionary. New York: Citadel, 1962.

Adams, Joey. Encyclopedia of Humor. New York: Bobb-Merrill Co., 1968.

Adams, Joey. Son of Encyclopedia of Humor. New York: Bobbs-Merrill Co., 1970.

Adler, Larry. Jokes and How to Tell Them. New York: Doubleday, 1963.

Allen, Steve. The Funny Men. New York: Simon and Schuster, 1956.

Allen, Steve. Funny People. New York: Stein and Day, 1981.

Allen, Steve. More Funny People, New York: Stein and Day, 1982.

Allen, Steve. How To Be Funny. Steve Allen with Jane Wollman. New York: McGraw Hill, 1987

Asimov, Isaac. Treasury of Humor. Boston: Houghton-Mifflin, 1971.

Berle, Milton. Milton Berle's Private Joke File. New York: Crown Publishers, Inc., 1989.

Blakely, James "Doc". Handbook of Wit & Pungent Humor. Houston: Rich Publishing, 1980.

Blakely, James "Doc". Push Button Wit. Houston: Rich Publishing, 1986.

Bonham, Tal D. Another Treasury of Clean Jokes. Nashville: Broadman Press, 1983.

Braude, Jacob M. The Treasury of Wit and Humor. Englewood Cliffs: Prentice-Hall, 1964.

Braude, Jacob M. Handbook of Humor for All Occasions. Englewood Cliffs: Prentice-Hall, 1958.

Braude, Jacob M. Speaker's Encyclopedia of Stories. Englewood Cliffs: Prentice-Hall.

Buescher, Walter M. Walter Buescher's Library of Humor. Englewood Cliffs, N.J.: Prentice-Hall, Inc., 1984.

Byrne, Robert. The Other 637 Best Things Anybody Ever Said. New York: Atheneum, 1984.

Carter, Judy. Stand Up Comedy The Book. New York: Dell, 1989.

Cerf, Bennett. Fifteen Joke Collections. New York: Doubleday, 1944-1972.

Copeland, Lewis & Faye. 10,000 Jokes, Toasts & Stories. New York: Garden City, 1965.

Dickson, Paul. Jokes. New York: Delacorte Press, 1984.

Esar, Evan. The Humor of Humor. New York: Bramhall House, 1953.

Esar, Evan. 20,000 Quips and Quotes. New York: Doubleday, 1968.

Esar, Evan. The Comic Encyclopedia. New York: Doubleday, 1978.

Esar, Evan. Esar's Comic Dictionary. New York: Doubleday, 1983.

Fechtner, Leopold. 5,000 One & Two Liners for Any & Every Occasion. West Nyack: Parker Pub., 1973.

Fechtner, Leopold. Encyclopedia of Ad-libs, Insults & Wisecracks. West Nyack: Parker Publishing, 1977.

Fechtner, Leopold. Galaxy of Funny Gags, Puns, Quips & Putdowns. West Nyack: Parker Publishing, 1980.

Fisher, Russ. In Search of the Funny Bone. Houston, Texas: Rich Publishing Company, 1988.

Gerler, William R. Executives Treasury of Humor For Every Occasion. West Nyack: Parker, 1965.

Helitzer, Melvin. Comedy Techniques for Writers & Performers. Athens, OH: Lawhead Press, 1984.

Helitzer, Melvin. Comedy Writing Techniques. Cincinnati: Writer's Digest, 1987.

Humes, James. C. Instant Eloquence. New York: Harper & Row, 1973.

Humes, James C. Podium Humor. New York: Harper & Row, 1975.

Jessel, George. You Too Can Make A Speech. New York: Grayson, 1956.

Jessel, George. The Toastmaster General's Guide To Successful Public Speaking. New York: Hawthorn Books, 1969.

Kearney, Paul W. Toasts and Anecdotes. New York: Grosset & Dunlap, 1923.

Klein, Allen. The Healing Power of Humor. Los Angeles: Jeremy P. Tarcher, Inc., 1989.

Klein, Allen. Quotations to Cheer You Up When the World Is Getting You Down. New York: Sterling Publishing Co. Inc. 1991.

Kushner, Malcolm. The Light Touch. How to Use Humor For Business Success. New York: Simon & Schuster, 1990.

Lieberman, Gerald F. 3,500 Good Jokes for Speakers. New York: Doubleday, 1975.

Lieberman, Gerald F. 3,500 Good Quotes for Speakers. New York: Doubleday, 1983.

Mahony, Patrick. Barbed Wit & Malicious Humor. Washington D.C.: Institute For The Study of Man.

McManus, Ed & Bill Nichols. We're Roasting Harry Tuesday Night. Englewood Cliffs: Prentice-Hall, 1984.

Orben, Robert. Complete Comedian's Encyclopedia Volumes I, II, III, IV, V and VI. New York: Lou Tannen, 1951-1959.

Orben, Robert. Encyclopedia of One-Liner Comedy. New York: Doubleday, 1966.

Orben, Robert. 2,100 Laughs for All Occasions. New York: Doubleday, 1982.

Pasta, Elmer, The Complete Book of Roasts, Boasts, and Toasts. West Nyack, New York: Parker Publishing Co., 1982.

Pendleton, Winston K. Complete Speaker's Galaxy of Funny Stories, Jokes, and Anecdotes. West Nyack, New York: Parker Publishing, 1979.

Perret, Gene. How to Write and Sell Humor. Cincinnati: Writer's Digest Books, 1982.

Perret, Gene. How to Hold Your Audience with Humor Cincinnati: Writer's Digest Books, 1984.

Perret, Gene. Using Humor For Effective Business Speaking, 1989.

Perret, Gene and Linda. Funny Business: Speakers Treasury of Business Humor For All Occasions. Englewood Cliffs, New Jersey: Prentice Hall, 1990.

Peter, Laurence J., and Bill Dana. The Laughter Prescription. New York: Ballantine Books, 1982.

Prochnow, Herbert V. & Son. A Dictionary of Wit, Wisdom & Satire. New York: Harper & Row.

Prochnow, Herbert V. & Son. New Guide for
    Toastmasters and Speakers. New York: Prentice-
    Hall, 1956.
Prochnow, Herbert V. & Son. The Public Speaker's
    Treasure Chest. New York: Harper & Row, 1977.
Rosten, Leo. Giant Book of Laughter. New York: Crown,
    1985.
Saks, Sol. The Craft of Comedy Writing. Cincinnati:
    Writer's Digest, 1985.
Schock, Al. Jokes For All Occasions. No. Hollywood,
    California: Wilshire Book Co., 1976.
Schutz, C.E. Political Humor. Cranbury, N.J.
    Associated University Presses, 1977.
Weisman, Israel H. Pulpit Treasury of Wit and Humor.
    New York: Prentice-Hall.
Wilde, Larry. See Books By Author.
Woods, Ralph L. The Modern Handbook of Humor.
    New York: McGraw-Hill, 1967.
Youngman, Henny. Take My Jokes, Please. New York:
    Richardson and Snyder, 1983.
Youngman, Henny. The Encyclopedia Of One Liners
    Katonah, NY: Ballymote, Inc. 1989.

ABOUT THE AUTHOR

Larry Wilde is a leading motivational humorist and seminar leader who speaks to major corporations, associations and healthcare facilities nationwide on the value of laughter. His programs demonstrate how successful individuals harness humor to relieve stress and achieve greater productivity.

This is the 50th book by Mr. Wilde, whom *The New York Times* has called, "America's best-selling humorist." His "Official" joke books have sold more than 11 million copies — the largest-selling series of its kind in publishing history. In addition, he produced two highly regarded works on comedy technique, *The Great Comedians Talk About Comedy* and *How the Great Comedy Writers Create Laughter* which are used as college textbooks.

Prior to his careers as humorist and author, he was a stand-up comedian and actor who appeared in major night clubs and on national television in commercials, sit-coms and talk shows.

Larry Wilde is the founder of National Humor Month, which begins on April Fools Day.

He lives on the Northern California coast with his wife, Maryruth, who is also an author.